Make It Relevant!

Strategies to Nurture, Develop, and Inspire Young Learners

VALERIE E. KING

■SCHOLASTIC

DEDICATION

For my Littles
—DR. KING

Editor: Maria L. Chang
Cover design by Tannaz Fassihi
Cover illustration by Michelle Haiyun Deng
Interior design by Maria Lilja
Photos © Shutterstock.com (4, 16, 62, 93). All other photos provided by author.

ISBN: 978-1-338-76407-9
Scholastic Inc., 557 Broadway, New York, NY 10012
Copyright © 2022 by Valerie E. King
Published by Scholastic Inc. All rights reserved.
Printed in the U.S.A.
First printing, January 2022

1 2 3 4 5 6 7 8 9 10   40   31 30 29 28 27 26 25 24 23 22

CONTENTS

Why Does Relevance Matter?

To engage children, teachers must identify and capitalize on what's relevant in students' lives.

Something happened to me many years ago that nudged me to think about being relevant with children and for children. You see, I planned what I thought was an amazing literacy lesson. I used a song as a hook for the lesson and embedded all the important vocabulary and concepts within its lyrics. As I started to play the song, I looked out at my third graders—and they all stared at me blankly. I continued with the song until this eerie feeling crept over me. I couldn't tell if I felt disappointed or bewildered. In any case, I stopped the song after the first chorus and asked my learners, "Don't you all know this song?" They shook their heads in unison. Incredulously, I repeated, "You do not know this song?" And then I realized—not only was I *old*, but what I intended to use as a hook for my learners had no relevance to them. I was relying on my old habits, my creature comforts—instead of my learners' personal contexts.

The song? I'd be dating myself if I shared it. What matters is that for this lesson, I used a theme song from a situation comedy that aired from 1969 to 1974 . . . a few decades before my learners were even born. Whether it is a song, a book, a topic, or an idea, there is probably something that you share with your learners right now that leaves them absolutely disconnected. Or maybe something else is already stifling learning in your classroom.

It's funny now, but that was a turning point for me. I realized right then that if I am unable to identify and capitalize on what's relevant in my learners' lives and rely only on what I think is important, I have no chance of ever reaching them.

Keeping up with what is relevant—especially with little people—is a challenge.

Life is harried, and it is becoming more complex. Keeping up with what is relevant—especially with little people—is a challenge. My oldest learners are 8 years old. This age group typically is eager to learn. They are curious, and they question. It is imperative that we cultivate these innate learning traits and bring relevance to our learners.

Think for a moment about the teachers who made learning relevant for you. For me, it was Mrs. McDonald. Sophia Romano. Ronald Delivuk. Altos Godfrey. Kitty Niebuhr. Lee Doebler. Ann Hamilton. Sharon Compton. Jack Riley. You won't see any of these names decorating a star on the Hollywood Walk of Fame. They aren't engraved on a Pulitzer. Mrs. McDonald introduced me to Mr. P. Mooney, who taught me how to read. Sophia Romano let me write a poem based on a song that I loved and allowed me to bring in the record and play it for the class. Mr. Delivuk—I was in his science class the day the space shuttle *Challenger* exploded. Altos Godfrey taught me what it was like to develop film, to see something your eye sees from behind a lens come to life. Kitty Niebuhr had me reread *Bridge to Terabithia* as an adult and recognize that Terabithia can exist. Lee Doebler gave me my first and only B and made me feel that I was the same person before the B as after the B . . . and that there was more to learning than a grade. Ann Hamilton never spoke above a whisper and encouraged us to "lean in" when she spoke. Sharon Compton let me observe a rose beetle go from larva to pupa to beetle and was there to discover that someone vandalized our classroom and glued these creatures to our classroom chalkboard. She was also there when I failed a social studies test and signed my dad's name to it. And there was Dr. Jack Riley, who simply encouraged me to "invent myself."

These are the names of my teachers—educators who, like us, work tirelessly to impart knowledge and ignite thinking. But these teachers also illustrated the importance of building relationships. They knew that to build a relationship with me, they had to seek the matters that were relevant to me. I may not recall all the specifics of what I learned from each of them, but I do remember how they turned every piece of learning into an opportunity to explore something relevant. It was the little things these teachers did that made the biggest difference. I believe teachers need to embrace the little opportunities to be relevant with their learners. One can easily imagine having a conversation with a high school senior about politics, climate change, or humanitarian issues. I advocate that these same conversations and ideas, as well as many more, also address the concerns and abilities of young learners and must be pervasive learning points in "little" classrooms. Thus, the birth of *Make It Relevant! Strategies to Nurture, Develop, and Inspire Young Learners*.

> *It was the little things these teachers did that made the biggest difference.*

NUDGE TO RELEVANCE

- **What do you remember as most significant about your teachers?**
- **What would your learners say is most significant about you?**

ONE

What Is Relevance?

Webster's dictionary defines *relevance* as "the quality or state of being closely connected or appropriate." This definition suggests that if we connect appropriately with our learners, we create relevance. It's a great notion, but it seems to be missing the "oomph" that relevance requires of educators. If we think big picture—how we as educators want to make an impact on our learners—the term *significant* more closely mimics the relevance we need to establish. Think about it: In today's information-rich world, teachers are no longer "holders of knowledge" as we once were. If we aren't careful and don't continue to become relevant to our learners, we as education professionals are going to lose our worth. As educators, we have the obligation to be relevant in our learners' lives— to both a cognitive and an affective stance.

How do you connect with and make an impact on your learners?

The Mindset List, created at Beloit College in 1998 and now researched and produced at Marist College, is a testament to how rapidly relevance can change. This annual list, which started out as a witty reminder to higher-education colleagues to watch their references, explores "the cultural touchstones and experiences that have shaped the worldview of students," particularly those who are entering college in the fall (Beloit College, 2014). For our purposes, consider how today's littlest learners are entering a world in which:

- the pound sign on the phone is known as "hashtag"
- celebrity "selfies" are far cooler than autographs
- there has always been TV designed to be watched exclusively on the web
- their screens keep getting smaller as their parents' screens grow ever larger
- they no longer need to ask for directions to get someplace; they simply need an address, thanks to GPS
- many of their favorite feature films have always been largely, if not totally, computer-generated
- USB ports are as familiar as wall sockets
- they have always lived in cyberspace
- they have never seen an airplane "ticket"
- they can't imagine people carrying luggage through the airport—they only see them rolling suitcases
- Amazon is not just a river in South America

When you scan this list or think about the concepts shared in this book, I hope it's with a sense of "I never thought of that before." In today's classrooms, educators may sometimes feel out of touch with their learners. Instead of struggling through a teaching season of disconnect, we need to marvel at how rapidly the world changes and figure out how we can invite that ever-evolving world into our classrooms.

NUDGE TO RELEVANCE

- **What ideas or thoughts do your learners share that make you feel out of touch with their world?**

Why Relevance Matters

And though she be but little, she is fierce.
—SHAKESPEARE

I call my learners "Littles." When I initially established this moniker, it was merely to set my learners apart from other students, because the needs of the littlest learners are sometimes as quirky as they are themselves. Then, being one of the "Littles" became really cool. Every year I tell my group of learners that many people think that little children can't do very much. Of course, I am just teasing them, but they *love* it. My learners have adopted and adapted Shakespeare's quote: "And though she be but little, she is fierce." This quote represents all the Littles, not just the female learners in my classroom. In fact, all I have to say at any time is, "We are but little . . ." and they respond with a resounding chorus, "but we are FIERCE!" I suppose that's what being relevant means—helping children find their voice through what matters to them. In effect, it also means finding your teaching voice through what matters to your learners.

Being relevant means helping children find their voice through what matters to them.

It wasn't so long ago that a global pandemic altered the context of education overnight. We faced many challenges, but navigating the challenges also gave cause for celebration. The moments we celebrated were influenced by relevant matters. Suddenly, it was clear that educators' intent mattered much more than the content.

While educators have defined frameworks to teach and a set of standards to bind the learning in our classrooms, we need to consider six tenets as we focus on being relevant with our learners, no matter the curriculum or the learning context. We need to:

- Lean in
- Improve understanding
- Tackle emotionality
- Treasure culture
- Look around
- Explore experiences

I have been practicing and scrutinizing these tenets for more than 20 years in countless classrooms and among many, many learners. My commitment to these ideas helps my Littles and me make the classroom a joyful place of learning. The matters that are relevant to young learners are enduring. In fact, even during the COVID-19 pandemic of 2020, when education had to react with immediacy, it was these matters that held. These tenets ensured that learning continued, but with more relevance to the situation at hand.

The matters that are relevant to young learners are enduring.

Through personal anecdotes from two decades of teaching and individual and professional interactions, both in and out of the field of education, the chapters in this book offer ideas to reflect on as you consider your own teaching relevance and why it is crucial for today's young learners to thrive. In addition, you'll also find a collection of relevant lessons at the back of this book. These lessons are by no means exhaustive. Instead, consider them as a place to begin framing relevant matters in your classroom. These lessons are anchored in literature and require few materials. They provoke questioning and inspire reflection. They are curated to offer room for teacher adaptation and personalization, as they relate to your learners. After all, that is what being relevant demands.

NUDGE TO RELEVANCE

- How can your learners identify with you in a meaningful, substantive way?
- Where will you begin your journey to being relevant with your learners?

TWO

Belonging, Believing, Becoming
A Framework for Relevance

From sharing literature to conducting science experiments to investigating primary documents and artifacts, educators can harness the power of relevance. It is the single constant that can supersede curriculum. Relevance is an idea that promotes connectedness, comfortable curiosity, and social-emotional confidence. Many countries, in their zeal to broaden and improve young children's learning, have developed guidelines, standards, curricula, or similar documents to communicate and support the importance of early learning. Much of this work, however, treats relevance as an abstract concept; relevance can be nebulous and challenging to commit to a guiding document. While a significant part of the effort on these guiding documents has been completed in the last decade, it is Australia's Early Years Learning Framework that first raised the possibility of educators' establishing a structure for relevance.

The Council of Australian Governments, specifically the Department of Education, Employment, and Workplace Relations (2009), developed the Early Years Learning Framework to support educators in their effort to "provide young children with opportunities to maximize their potential and develop a foundation for future success in learning" (p. 5). More broadly, the hope is that with this guiding document, learners will become "successful, confident, creative, and active and informed citizens" (p. 5). While the framework is explicit about pedagogy and methodologies, its underpinning is the notion that as educators we must view children's lives as characterized by belonging, being, and becoming (DEEWR, 2009). With a nod to the work in Australia, this outlook has become an integral part of my personal learning and teaching as it relates to identifying and focusing on what matters most for young learners.

After many conversations with educators and children, coupled with a reflective glance at anecdotal situations in my classroom, I expanded this framework into a philosophy from which I set my standards, my approaches to curriculum, the culture I create, and my support of my students' social-emotional learning. The concept of engagement and building strong relationships to create connectedness defines **belonging**. In my practice, the idea of "being" and establishing a sense of here and now, as well as a sense of self for children easily translates into **believing** in oneself. Changing the characteristic of *being* to one of *believing* is more than just a conceptual vocabulary shift. Young learners' belief in their own abilities has a profound effect in classrooms on a social-emotional and academic level. The idea of believing prompts learners to establish a sense of comfortable curiosity while embracing a genuine self-awareness. Finally, giving children every opportunity to use their voice helps build their social confidence and shape who they are to **become**. These ideals of belonging, believing, and becoming helped shape the framework for creating and maintaining relevance in my classroom.

Relevance is not simply built on an awareness of trends our young learners connect with.

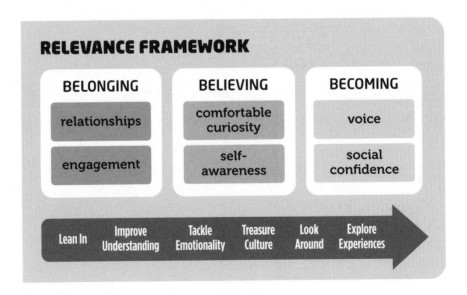

It may seem ironic to utilize a framework built around relevance given the shifting nature of significant themes in our world. It is important to understand that relevance is not simply built on an awareness of trends our young learners connect with. Rather, we establish relevance by building relationships, providing opportunities for engagement, fostering a comfortable curiosity, supporting self-awareness, and creating space that honors student voice in order to build self-confidence.

Each of the tenets at the bottom of the Relevance Framework is woven into the broader outcomes we want in our young learners—the opportunity to belong, believe, and become. When educators make a commitment to lean in, improve understanding, tackle emotionality, treasure culture, look around, and explore experiences with young learners, they will be able to reach and teach their students in a more relevant manner. While the following chapters present each tenet in isolation, teachers must weave these beliefs throughout every interaction with their young learners to establish relevance. When these beliefs have a stronghold in the classroom, teachers establish a context for learning in which young learners belong, believe, and become.

Before we explore the practical application of the ideas in this book, let me introduce each of these broader concepts and share why they are important to develop in our young learners.

Belonging

To create a sense of belonging in the classroom, teachers need to lean in and provide both unspoken and voiced, wholehearted, implicit understanding of young learners. Young learners must be exposed to an engaging classroom environment punctuated by an inclusive culture that strengthens individuality. When educators lean in, they establish, nourish, and maintain relationships with their learners. These relationships are built on teachers' creating intentional opportunities for learners to feel they belong. Learners thus move from simply feeling "I am part of a classroom community and I belong here" to a refined sense of believing in themselves, appreciating others' differences, and celebrating their individuality within a broader culture. This subtle transfer of confidence enables young learners to shape their social-emotional awareness and build a comfortable curiosity with learning processes, some of which highlight failures over successes and use small, real-world backgrounds and situations to further build relevance.

Create intentional opportunities for children to feel they belong in your classroom community.

Establishing relationships is an investment toward a sense of belonging. Educators believe relationships matter, but how perceptive are we at building relationships with our learners? Do we encourage learners to build relationships with one another? Are our efforts primarily authentic and simulated only when the authenticity is impossible? Are relationships so prevalent in our classroom that every single young learner could exclaim, "Yes, I belong here!"? If you cannot answer emphatically, "Of course!" then you need to address the little things that can promote human connectedness in your students. Fostering a sense of belonging in young learners assures a context in which learning can thrive as it obligates children to believe in themselves.

Believing

Believing in oneself is an abstract concept, especially for young learners. Establishing a growth mindset and promoting young learners' agency, or ownership of their learning, are cornerstones to strengthening belief. We need to help young learners cultivate an awareness of their being, especially regarding emotions. In my experience, social-emotional learning is analogous to on-the-job training. It must be authentic above all, and it must be personalized. Much is written about social-emotional learning. While the research has merit, lessons designed to address social-emotional needs are often implemented in isolation. Social-emotional learning must be pervasive. Every lesson has the potential for a social or emotional aspect to be embedded in it. Affective learning must evolve as a ubiquitous part of classroom life, highlighted by the cognitive and social experiences of our learners.

Children are emotional. Tackling emotionality begins with *accepting* the fact that young learners are going to be emotional. We have all had that young person in our room who cried for a seemingly insignificant reason, at least from our adult perspective. Young learners need a wide berth to experience emotions that coincide with learning in our classrooms. We can build experiences by *acknowledging* the emotions our young learners illustrate—the second approach to tackling emotionality. As young learners emote, we can design learning from those emotions. Finally, *addressing* the emotions that young learners exhibit in our classrooms in ways that don't force compliance is also important. Emotions are a natural outgrowth of being human. Classrooms are humanistic contexts. There are discoverable patterns of emotions in young learners. As educators, when we lean in, we grow more astute at addressing specific emotions so our learners become better equipped to regulate them.

When it comes to young learners, it is my experience that we too often focus on social-emotional ideas that are not relevant. This is partly due to the fact that we haven't taken the time to build relationships with our learners. We have not leaned in far enough to know what their hearts need. Each year, I focus on specific social-emotional principles, which include positivity, empathy, fairness, failure, resilience, and passion. They become living concepts throughout the year. These are not one-and-done ideas but rather beliefs that young learners can shape as they learn how to assimilate their thoughts, feelings, and actions. These ideas are, of course, not the only ones that exist with regard to social-emotional learning. Your classroom may have different needs. Your practice will define them. Even in my practice, some young learners need more time to dissect and assimilate a particular idea. The point is social-emotional needs warrant educators' intentional, specific, and unwavering attention. With a purposeful approach, young learners gain determination and spirit.

When teachers recognize and support young learners' social-emotional needs, children cultivate a social-emotional awareness that translates into confidence as they begin to tackle more challenging cognitive tasks. Finding a relevant place to tackle emotionality, young learners learn to embrace and accept emotions as a germane part of learning and use their emotions to an advantage. They learn to use their social-emotional self-awareness as a means to satisfy their thirst for learning without fear or reticence. Furthermore, social-emotional awareness leads to identifying similarities and celebrating differences as children learn to treasure culture. Through social-emotional awareness built on relevance, young learners are encouraged to recognize and get a broader sense of who they want to become.

Becoming

Educators of early learners have an incredible opportunity to embrace the power and potential of student voice—the impetus for establishing social confidence and clarity about who children want to become. Research points to the impact student voice has on learners in many areas, including social and emotional well-being (Dewey, 1916; Hattie, 2012; Mitra, 2008; Quaglia et al., 2020). Early learner classrooms are optimal settings to nurture student voice.

Developmentally, our earliest learners are curious and full of wonder. Young learners are egocentric; their world matters to them. They are persistent. They are opinionated. They are malleable. Along with all these characteristics, they are determined. We can capitalize on that small voice that says "me" when we introduce early learners to "we" by encouraging them to see their place within their learning. Not only must we recognize the power and potential of the littlest voices but also encourage it. It is critical for educators to embrace early learners' innate characteristics of wonder, ego, and curiosity and help them channel these so children can become their best selves. This is supported by providing a safe space for student voice to flourish. Each day, as children arrive in our classrooms, we have the opportunity to influence the conditions in the learning environment that either enhance or inhibit student voice. Early learning voice is a conduit to creation, innovation, and, more important, self-identity and worth. Therefore, silencing the voices of our littlest learners bars them from reaching their highest aspirations. In contrast, curating experiences that have a real-life purpose aimed at an authentic audience sets the stage for young learners to use their voice. Using their voice leads to social confidence that helps learners realize both their "here and now" and "then and when" potentials.

Encouraging children to use their voice helps promote creativity as well as self-confidence.

The unintentional default for teachers of young learners is to quiet student voice—not on purpose, but as a side effect of feeling the need to cover the curriculum or move the lesson along. Many educators simply cannot see the immediate relevance in student voice. Educators focus on the content of the voice, rather than the *intent* of the voice. Quaglia et al. (2020) suggest that fostering voice and creating a shared sense of responsibility in the classroom lead to increased engagement in learning.

Nurturing voice in our early learners can be accomplished with focus on becoming. There are specific approaches within the broader notion of student voice that teachers can put into practice to build a sense of belonging in young learners. These teacher behaviors include prioritizing listening over talking; seeing children as opportunities, not problems; shedding the "sage on the stage" persona; and boosting student responsibility and independence. When teacher behavior shifts to encourage student voice, authentic experiences are born.

THREE

Lean In

I Don't Understand and I Can't Explain

Creating relevant learning for Littles can seem daunting, given that every learning context is new and potentially unfamiliar for little learners. They enter the classroom with a myriad of school (and non-school) experiences. While I question my Littles a fair amount, I also lean in and listen to them. They get used to me listening intently to their commentary. I want them to feel the discomfort that often accompanies learning. I want them to rely on their own understanding and their own metacognition without me constantly interjecting.

Research highlights the influence of teacher voice in classrooms. Hattie's meta-analyses of research (2012) found that on average teachers talk for 70 to 80 percent of class time. His own research suggested an even higher 89 percent. Listening is a powerful tool in building independent and interdependent thinkers and learners. Listening also breaks teachers of the bad habit of talking too much.

While I tend to create a risk-free environment for everything that occurs in my classroom, my Littles know that if they don't understand something, they are responsible for asking for clarification. Many of my learners embrace this, while others still struggle with the assumptions that they should know everything and that not knowing is deemed a complete failure. Assure young learners that *not knowing* is actually success because it means they are on the cusp of learning something new! When my learners quite innocently share, "I don't understand," my default response used to be, "What don't you understand?" I can think of very few questions that sound more ridiculous than this one. If a learner knew how to explain what he or she didn't understand, then wouldn't that be a platform for the child to dissect the misunderstanding and puzzle it back together for learning? Eureka! "What don't you understand?" is the go-to phrase many educators use. I often hear this same refrain from other teachers in some form or another. I'm not sure if it is because we feel rushed or we have just never given it any thought.

Asking a learner what she already knows instead of what she does not know allows a teacher to pull from a relevant place.

Asking a learner, especially a Little, what he or she already knows instead of what he or she does *not* know allows a teacher to pull from a relevant place. It provides a building block to get to the important learning. What if we simply say, "Tell me what you already know," when a learner expresses confusion? Even if what he or she knows is a misconception or off topic, it can still reveal the next learning steps. I've shifted to this practice. While it is true that sometimes all my Littles know is how to write their name on their paper or that the holes go on the left side when formatting notebook paper—that's a start! Even building on that simple piece of knowledge has the potential to build relevance. Your next question could be, "What's next? Once your name is on your paper, what are you being asked to do?" This pattern becomes a dialogue of learning. Eventually the dialogue becomes a monologue, and learners begin to think more critically, dissect problems with prowess, and develop a belief in themselves.

To create those relationships that lead to relevance, we as teachers must dialogue with our learners. Asking children questions such as, "What do you know? What can you do? How did you get to this point? What is frustrating you? What were you thinking when you got stumped?" highlights an opportunity for learning. It also avoids the repetitive regurgitation of "I don't know" from our learners when we ask, "What don't you understand?" Children do not really know how to express what they don't know, so we have to draw that information out of them. If we invest in a learning dialogue instead of always relying on a quick check for understanding, children will begin to dissect their own thinking and push themselves further in learning.

NUDGE TO RELEVANCE

- What do you say when a child shares that he or she doesn't understand something?

- How can you create a learning dialogue in your classroom?

Relationships and Engagement

Engage your learners. Relationships matter. These statements are not new to education. When we pare down the idea of belonging, or establishing connectedness for our learners, it boils down to relationships and engagement. It is a misconception that *engagement* equals *entertainment*. Educators often falsely believe there is an expectation that every single lesson should be extraordinary. We also tend to measure the engagement factor by our learners' involvement. However, I believe that engagement is dependent on the educator or is at least a shared responsibility between the teacher and the learner. Engaged learners automatically connect to whatever is going on in the classroom. Sadly, we often excuse our responsibility to create joy in learning and suggest that a learner is not engaged because he or she lacks motivation. Engagement is teacher-driven. Not every lesson is going to be engaging to every learner. (I argue there is learning even in that situation.)

While some lessons do not present themselves as particularly engaging, we can consistently create a pleasing learning environment punctuated with experiences that create wonder and curiosity. I call these "mini engagements." Simply, if we focus on engaging our learners, we are obligated to create a context in which learners will participate. Often, we need reminding that student participation can look very different from one student to the next.

Offering novel resources stimulates curiosity and engages little learners.

Developmentally and culturally, how young learners engage is diverse. By establishing relationships with our learners and allowing an open space and expectation for peer relationships to evolve, we encourage a sense of belonging. Establishing a sense of belonging in young learners is not pushing them to become who we perceive they should be. Schools often prompt learners to "come out of your shell"—summarized by Cain (2012) as "that noxious expression which fails to appreciate that some animals naturally carry shelter everywhere they go, and that some humans are just the same" (p. 6). Share this analogy with learners to communicate, "You belong here as you are."

Little things within your classroom can immediately set the tone for building relationships and engagement.

The sense of belonging, or lack thereof, begins as soon as a young learner arrives at the threshold of the classroom. Little things within your classroom can immediately set the tone for building relationships and engagement. Simply, lean in.

Lean Into Classroom Expectations

Move away from teacher-centered rules. Move away from teacher ego. Move toward student voice and student agency. Young learners have a keen perception of expectations. Discuss commitments and how collective commitments in a classroom allow for interdependence. A small shift, such as using vocabulary words and expressions with intention, can establish a strong sense of belonging. Think about approaching even the sticky moments with a positive vernacular. Consider the difference and the message each of these statements communicates:

- "Here are the rules for our classroom this year . . ."
- "I invite you to think about what is important to your learning in our classroom this year. Together we are going to commit to having the best year ever."

Setting expectations collaboratively promotes responsibility, agency, and community in our young learners. Even with a collaborative approach, the message is clear: "You belong here, your ideas matter, you have a place in this community."

Before sharing your expectations for your learners, flip the script. Ask your students, "What do you expect from me?" It's a vulnerable place, but you will be delighted and surprised by some of the responses: "Tell funny jokes." "Use big words." Such small requests become details in the fabric of my classroom community. I am a horrible joke teller, but I model risk-taking by finding jokes to share with my Littles. "Use big words" I can master. I am always sharing a term with multiple synonyms, from various languages or cultures. I may never have considered these things if I had set classroom expectations with blinders on. I believe if one of our learners communicates something, it is important to him or her. If we, as teachers, always take this stance, we'll learn valuable things about our students.

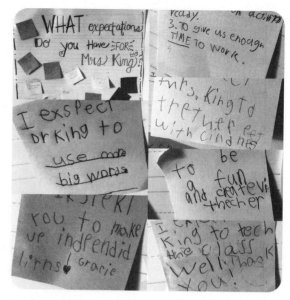

My learners' expectations of me

As you set expectations for your classroom, do you also set expectations for yourself? Teaching is an opportunity to be reflective. Every single year, I share my personal teaching manifesto. I dissect the word *manifesto* and lean into my Littles as I explain that it means my declaration of who I am going to be as a teacher. It is my promise to them, and it keeps me centered on what matters. In turn, I guide my Littles to create their own learning manifestos. They each share their thoughts. We look for patterns in the expectations: categories that encompass our community expectations. We then create a class manifesto—a promise that we display in a prominent place. Rather than a list of prescribed rules that miss out on relevant matters, we have a living expectation, created with trusting relationships (and sometimes a lot of extra words) that we can all commit to support.

Lean Into Choice

Marzano et al. (2010) claim that allowing for choice in the classroom increases engagement and gives the perception to students that the learning tasks have more meaning. I believe this to be true. I also believe choice fosters student agency. By giving young learners choice, even guided choice, they connect more deeply to the task and are more invested in the learning process.

When it comes to offering choice in the classroom, especially one filled with young learners, the indecision can be challenging for both teachers and students. If you have ever observed little learners choosing from a selection of lunch entrees, you will understand how hard it is to stand alongside them and wait for them to decide. It is also quite possible to offer too much choice. However, there are ways teachers can incorporate choice for young learners.

Choice Seating

Lean into flexible seating. Even if you create one area in your classroom that dispenses with traditional seating, allow it to be a choice area. In recent years, I've flipped my school furniture to offer a more flexible, choice learning environment. I provide for small groups, partners, and even the "island seeker."

I model each learning space with a "do" and a "don't." For example, the stability yoga balls are always a hit, and I show my Littles how to use their core to stay still. I recite, "Seat and feet . . . I repeat, seat and feet . . . Don't you cheat." I show them how bums must touch the yoga ball and feet must touch the floor. Then I might say something like, "If you're wearing green today, go pick a seat." After the first day? I let children choose their seats as they come in and go directly to their collaborative choice work groups.

Let learners choose where they sit—even if it's not on a chair.

I do not use a rotating schedule for seating. Because of the implicit and explicit expectations we build in the classroom together, I don't ever have to schedule who sits where. Sometimes a Little's feelings might get hurt because his or her choice seat is occupied. A simple suggestion like, "I bet tomorrow you can try again," or "Have a conversation with a peer and see if you can advocate for yourself" works well. (Yes, I use the word *advocate*.) Another reason I don't use a rotating schedule is it sends the message that we are a teacher-centered classroom. We are not.

What happens if—or rather, *when*—a child uses use the seating inappropriately? Everyone gets a fair warning. Everyone gets one free shot to make a mistake. However, if someone decides to use the stability ball as a hop-along after a fair warning, he or she has to choose another seat. It's rare that this happens, but occasionally it does.

Choice Partners

I recognize that assigning groups and partners needs to be strategic at times. But it doesn't always have to be. There are many times learners should have the opportunity to work with whomever they want to work with. This was something I had to learn over time. I wanted to control who worked with whom. I wanted to make sure that more-capable learners weren't paired with less-capable learners and doing their work for them. Or I wanted to make sure I didn't have a group of three boys and one girl because . . . why?

But now, whenever I can, I allow learners to choose whom they work with. We spend time discussing teamwork and what it means. I use the terms *hijacker* and *hitchhiker*. A hijacker is someone who wants to take over a group learning context. This is a learner who does not collaborate, but wants to control everything that happens in the group, from process to product. In Littles' eyes, a hijacker is bossy. On the other hand, a hitchhiker is someone who does not do anything in a group learning context. In true hitchhiker fashion, these learners get a free learning journey. Hitchhikers do not contribute to the group's collaborative goal. They merely sit back and enjoy the ride. No one wants to be either. (I know those terms are not relevant for little learners, but I invite them into a brief flashback to my era.) We debrief partner and group work from an affective stance. What went well today with your group? What went poorly? And because I have leaned into these Littles in so many ways, we rarely have issues.

Choice Tasks and Products

There are a multitude of ways children can show what they have learned. Offer choice in the process. Let them choose how they show off their learning. Allow for product-differentiated choice, designed by your learners. If you are so inclined, offer a choice menu, but leave a free space for learner-designed choice. Provide choices that tap into the diversity in your classroom. Provide choices that explore technology. Provide choices that offer creativity. Set the criteria, and let learners choose how to meet that criteria. Do not limit their abilities.

Choice Texts

Let learners choose their texts. I hope the practice of limiting children's exposure to text and giving learners books to read is an archaic practice. Indeed, there are contexts in which a teacher needs to facilitate the text being used. In general, however, children have the innate ability to choose texts that are right for them. What if they choose something in which the text is too hard? They are going to recognize this. Certainly, if they don't recognize it, you will when you confer with them. What if it's too easy? Well, it goes back to what is relevant. I read voraciously. Sometimes I love to read easy texts. I reread books I like. So maybe a too-easy book doesn't address the concept or skill you want a learner to work on, but it does build voice and agency because you allowed that child to select his or her own text.

> *In general, children have the innate ability to choose texts that are right for them.*

While these are incremental ways you can explore building a choice environment in your classroom, there are opportunities for larger expressions of self-selection. Genius Hour, Passion Projects, and Problem-Based Learning scenarios can all have embedded choice options. Just ensure that you are fostering belonging by allowing your learners to make particular choices on their own.

Lean Into Learning Huddles

A new approach to morning work has made an appearance in classrooms. This approach dismisses worksheets and provides a more welcoming invitation to a young learner's day. Daniels (2017) defines *soft start* as "not rigid, but gentle, individualized, and peaceful beginnings, driven by personal choice, not ordained by someone else's agenda or requirements" (p. 61). This morning routine utilizes various tasks and materials, allowing young learners to participate with little if any interference from the teacher.

Curious, I decided to implement this routine prior to morning meetings in my classroom. I set aside 15 to 20 minutes at the beginning of each day to provide a consistent platform in which Littles lean into one another, collaborate, and often become necessary problem solvers— sometimes not just with the task at hand. I christened this part of the day "Learning Huddles," with the focus on collaborative work through choice. The term itself isn't insignificant. If you recall, "use big words" is an expectation my learners have of me. Using this opportunity to attend to a relevant matter they expressed and to promote vocabulary learning, I explain that a *huddle* is a small group of people gathered closely to strategize, plan, or problem solve together. I share illustrations of a football huddle or people huddling together to get warm to give concrete examples and to set expectations of the grouping during this learning time. (In prior years, I have used the terms "learning scrums" and "learning jams." Call them what you or your learners want but make the name purposeful.)

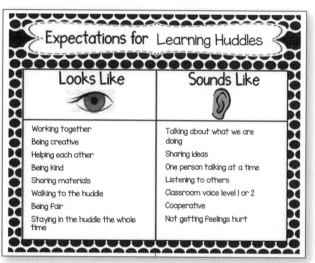

Looks Like	Sounds Like
Working together	Talking about what we are doing
Being creative	Sharing ideas
Helping each other	One person talking at a time
Being kind	Listening to others
Sharing materials	Classroom voice level 1 or 2
Walking to the huddle	Cooperative
Being fair	Not getting feelings hurt
Staying in the huddle the whole time	

Expectations for Learning Huddles

As a class, we set expectations for Learning Huddles based on my learners' experiences.

Activities for Learning Huddles can be anything you want them to be. They can be commercially crafted brain games, paper-and-pencil prompts, play dough, building bricks (e.g., Legos), or something as simple as a tub of plastic sea animals. Each of these can become a prompt for collaboration and problem solving, giving each learner a place of belonging. Explore what matters to your learners. Find trinkets, materials, images, or objects that connect to the curriculum. Be deliberate with what you provide, but do not narrow the experience. The tasks themselves should be strategic, and while they may be disguised as play, they should offer engaging challenges for young learners. They should also be intentional. The tasks can connect to a broader content understanding, but the intent is collaboration, problem solving, and interdependence.

I set up my classroom so that upon entering, learners see a display of the various Learning Huddles offered for the day, along with a description of each activity and a number depicting how many learners can collaborate on each huddle. Here are a few examples of my Littles' favorite Learning Huddles:

Metaphor Box In a box, place small items, such as a key, a seashell, miniature animal figurines, a raffle ticket, a penny (you get the idea). Pick an item and prompt Littles to share what that item represents. They will move from very concrete to more abstract ideas as they practice. One example that stands out to me is a small dollhouse mop. When I used this example with educators, I got responses such as "dirty, cleanliness, housework . . ." When I had this item in our class Metaphor

Box, one Little said, "evil." I was surprised—and curious. Upon further prompting, he explained, "It made me think of Cinderella, and she had evil stepsisters that made her do the work." Through this task, young learners begin to understand figurative

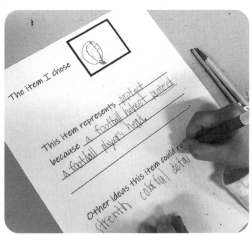

A learner picks an object from the Metaphor Box and explains what the object represents.

language. The thinking used during this task transfers into young learners' expressive speaking and writing repertoires as evidenced by their colorful and involved responses.

Lion in the Way Named after an idiom for an obstacle or danger, this is an ambiguous problem-solving task. Ambiguity offers a place for analysis and debate. Collect images from magazines or clip art that represent a setting or context with a predicament; for example, a road that has washed away, a parade in a rainstorm, a piano that needs to be lifted to the top floor of a building. Also collect images of random objects, such as a balloon, a sandwich, a piano, and so on. (Note: These suggestions are merely examples; this task is open-ended and can be shaped to suit your classroom. I find that real-life examples, though more intensive on the preparation side, work better.) To start, have each learner take an object image card. Then, present a setting or context card to the group and invite each learner to share how his or her object can help solve the predicament. Next, have learners work collaboratively and share how together their objects can solve the predicament. For example: How can a peanut butter and jelly sandwich help lift a piano to the top of a high-rise building? "Well, the man doing the work. You know, the one lifting it up? Well, if he's hungry, he can eat his sandwich just sitting, waiting for a friend to come help him." (Penny, age 7)

Jigsaw Puzzles Not surprisingly, young learners develop many physical, cognitive, and social-emotional skills as they explore jigsaw puzzles. For example:

- They learn to group pieces by color or pattern.
- As they explore sides and shapes, emergent geometry becomes part of a collaborative conversation.
- They get practice in visual-spatial reasoning as they transfer the image to the concrete puzzle pieces.
- They experience keen satisfaction, knowing there is a foreseeable end to puzzle solving.
- As they work on puzzles for several weeks, they practice collaboration on a large process task.
- They celebrate when they complete a puzzle.

Learners create a mosaic by putting together solved 2x2 Rubik's Cubes.

Rubik's Cube As a veteran educator, I'm delighted when trends that I experienced as a young learner make it back into popular culture and I can find a way to bring them into the classroom. The multicolored Rubik's Cube is one such example. The cubes come in various sizes, including 2x2 and 3x3. Using one of these smaller versions, young learners can work independently to twist and turn the sides of the cube to create a solid color on at least one face. (You can find online videos that offer step-by-step solutions to various Rubik's Cubes.) Afterward, learners can work collaboratively and combine their cubes to create a picture or mosaic.

Loose Parts Play This is one of our Learning Huddle choices that offer the highest level of imagination, adaptation, and interaction. Later in this chapter, I explore the theory behind "loose parts" and the learning discovery that this open-ended, adult-removed exploration prompts in young learners (page 33).

With My Hands Using the book *With My Hands: Poems About Making Things,* by Amy Ludwig VanDerwater, as a jumping-off point, learners explore making things. They read a poem and answer prompts that I leave with the materials. Poems about soap carvings, collage, origami, and shadows motivate young thinkers to create the things suggested by the prompt.

Learning Huddles is a sacred time for teachers to watch. Recognize that leaning in does not equal talking; more often, leaning in is watching and waiting and giving space to allow the needs of your learners to evolve. My Littles do not defer to me for support—this is built into the expectation in our classroom. They are accustomed to my refrain: "You are an amazing problem solver. This is a problem-solving classroom. What can you do?" At times, peers will help dissect a situation. However, everyone is aware that they have a limited time for Learning Huddles. Learners rationalize that the more time it takes to figure out a space, the less time there is to engage in it.

Let me share an incident that happened one time during Learning Huddles that highlights the importance of giving children space and time to explore learning freely. I watched as one of my "opportunity learners" (you know the ones who always take the opportunity to ruffle expectations, just slightly) lingered by a particular table that featured building bricks (i.e., Legos). In this Learning Huddle, children read a poem and use the building bricks to respond to a prompt. This Little did not get to his chosen huddle before the maximum number of children convened at the worktable. I could almost tell what he was thinking as he evaluated the scene: *Do I . . .*

1. *advocate for myself and see if someone will swap places with me?*
2. *exhibit some emotionality and work through the moment?*
3. *or . . . ?* (Because sometimes Littles are not predictable at all!)

This Little Learner picked number 3. The details are not important, but he did not react within the expectation we had set. Since I have established that Learning Huddles are not teacher-centric, I allowed him the space to show his feelings. After enduring several minutes of groans and alligator tears and some shameful looks toward me, a peer went up to him and offered him her space. I wanted to intervene, but because I believe so strongly in leaning in and letting learners establish their own relationships, I simply watched. The emotional Little swapped places and all was right in his world.

I didn't let this go unnoticed. When we completed our huddles and transitioned to morning meeting, I expressed what I observed and shared this example of being kind and gracious. I emphasized that the lesson here is that when people do things like that for us, we should always pay it forward. My Littles seemed to understand, but as teachers we always live in hope for that moment of transfer. Well, it happened. The very next week, I watched this same emotional Little go up to his peer and say, "Since you let me have your spot last week, you can have my spot this week. Thank you." Would this moment stick forever? Maybe not. But it was a definite exclamation mark to leaning in and the important hidden social-emotional learning that was happening in a cognitive context.

The social conversation and interdependence children derive from these low-prep, high-appeal, limited-time-commitment tasks highlight the power of relationships and authentic engagement. From my Littles' anecdotal remarks, Learning Huddles are a huge hit. My Littles share consistent positive reviews about them:

- "You can be creative! There are no limits in Learning Huddles." (Abigayle, age 7)

- "You can play and learn at the same time." (Viktor, age 7)

- "I like collaborating because other people have different ideas." (Aahana, age 7)

- "You can express yourself and know that not everyone is the same." (Helen, age 7)

Lean Into a Consistent Morning Meeting

If you have not established a consistent, purposeful space to meet with your learners every single day, consider the possibilities. Morning meetings were first established "by Northeast Foundation for Children staff as part of the Responsive Classroom approach to teaching and learning" (Kriete & Bechtel, 2002, p. 4). The Responsive Classroom approach provides a specific structure with components that can be integrated into the morning meeting time. However, there is no hard and fast rule on what the meetings should look like. I advocate that if you are truly being relevant with your learners, then design the expectation for morning meetings together with them. In my classrooms through the years, the structure has been very similar. They consist of a greeting, an "upside" share time (more on this below), breaking news, a look ahead at our day, and a class cheer, class song, or some sort of hook to get our day started.

Here are some of the benefits to morning meetings:

- **Morning meetings create trust in our classroom.** Littles rush to close the doors so that no one can overhear our conversations.

- **Morning meetings give all children the opportunity to feel important.** Morning meetings are a natural platform in which every learner has the opportunity to share. Whether you provide a specific theme for sharing, such as a favorite animal or what they did over the holiday, or offer a simple greeting involving the entire group, every learner feels heard and celebrated.

- **Morning meetings promote social-emotional confidence.**
  Littles share. Let's face it: Littles overshare, given the chance.
  My morning meeting time allows a space for sharing. Several
  years ago, a radio host I was listening to shared his thoughts
  on gratitude and how writing down one thing every day
  created a mostly positive context for him when things were
  less than terrific. I wondered if this same approach would work
  with young learners. Could we use a consistent, reflective time
  each day to identify the "upside" or the silver lining to some
  sticky situations? We could. We have. We do. My learners
  have a small journal in which to write about a situation that
  didn't go their way at home or at school or on the ball field.
  But they also have to reflect on what they learned from that
  situation or how there was still something good and positive
  in the situation. (See page 59 for more about the Upside
  Journal.) We use time during our morning meetings to share
  our upsides. We help one another see positives when we
  can't think of one. In short, the moments of sharing become
  real-life social-emotional learning. Ironically, my Littles have
  moved from "I was upset I didn't get the toy I wanted, but at
  least I got something" to "We lost our ball game 10−0, but at
  least it gave me good practice."

- **Morning meetings provide preparation and expectation
  for the day's learning.** A schedule and predictable routine
  for young children create a framework of confidence and
  reassurance, thus leading to self-assurance and a keener sense
  of belonging. This self-confidence promotes a greater sense
  of discovery. In turn, the greater awareness of discovery leads
  to believing in oneself. Our learners benefit so much when we
  provide them a daily, consistent format of the day's learning.

Lean Into Play

Play disguised as learning is often a provocative topic in education.
It appears that the content in school curriculum sometimes fails to
recognize intent. Christakis (2017) suggests, "Child's play . . . falls into
a huge category of supposedly natural behavior that is actually quite
hard to accomplish without intention and assistance" (p. 140). When
we are intentional about play and trust the research, it can be a force in
engaging little learners and establishing relationships. For example, play
allows for choice, problem solving, and collaboration. Gray (2011) and
Lynch (2015) further suggest that play allows children to practice joy, get

along, commiserate, and shed ego. By its very definition, play facilitates creativity, innovation, resourcefulness, and originality. Learning Huddles are intricately designed as play. The elements of choice, problem solving, and collaboration are the key components of this learning experience.

A more intentional integration of play, as introduced in ideas for Learning Huddles, is that of "Loose Parts Play" (see page 28).

By its very definition, play facilitates creativity, innovation, resourcefulness, and originality.

Nicholson (2009) developed a theory based on a belief that "loose parts" in our environment—materials that can be moved around, combined, reshaped, or manipulated in various ways—empower creativity. His work focused on the design of children's learning environments or areas where children naturally convene. His learning principles emphasized allowing children to play with an interdisciplinary approach. Furthermore, Nicholson recommended creating a repository of resources to support learning strategies when children are engaged in this type of play. Educators have applied and translated Nicholson's theory and principles to establish deliberate opportunities for play in their classrooms. A simple internet search of "loose parts play" reveals a plethora of ideas, including materials, prompts, and suggestions. The importance of this play experience is to remember that the best learning comes from objects that allow learners to play in many ways. Loose Parts Play in my classroom evolved into an engaging, focused opportunity for creative exploration.

I started our Loose Parts collection on a school-ground hike. Each carrying a bag, my Littles collected natural objects, such as pine cones, sticks, acorns, and stones, to fill our Loose Parts containers. As its name suggests, Loose Parts are loosely defined; they can be natural or synthetic. We use a myriad of materials. In fact, Littles have taken to collecting bottle caps and pull tabs and random junk-drawer finds. While the materials are loosely defined, I create planned prompts for the interactions. Some might argue that this is a slight detour from the pure intent of loose play, but setting a purpose makes a solid defense for using play in our classrooms. Using these prompts, my Littles choose their materials and create.

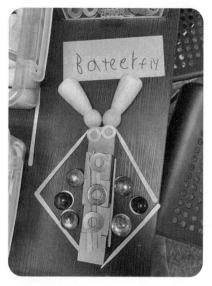

Providing a prompt for how to use the loose parts turns this "play" activity into an intentional learning experience.

Let Them Lean Into You, Too

If you were to ask your learners to write a biography about you, what would they say? If you were to ask them to list three things you love and three things you are unsure about, would they be able to do this? Teachers have barriers (unconscious ones, I hope) to letting learners lean into them. Creating a sense of belonging through a relationship with you does not have to be explicitly expressed. Your environment is a window to who you are. What touches of you are part of your classroom? What stories do you tell your learners about your life? How often do you model the struggle of learning? I have noticed that the more I participate in the learning alongside them, the more they lean in.

My Littles notice everything. I am reminded of a time when one of my Littles, Ben, said to me upon entering the classroom, "Wow! You look new today!" I wasn't sure what he meant and, of course, asked him just that. He said, "Well, you're wearing red lipstick today. You just look new. I mean, I can't say you look old, so that just means you look new." I thought how astute of this six-year-old to notice that I was wearing red lipstick. I am certain that many of you have had learners emulate your style, your words, or your behavior. When teachers allow their learners to lean in, what follows is a solid learning posture of belonging in each of them.

FOUR

Improve Understanding
It Is Not About the Shoes

While my educational career has led me to teaching the littlest of learners, I find it is necessary to engage in learning with the whole spectrum of students. Middle-grade and high-school educators can learn from primary and elementary learners and vice versa. Broadening your repertoire, which I discuss later in this book, is important. Sometimes the discussions we have with other educators can help strengthen our relevance with our own learners.

Recently I had a conversation with a friend who is a high-school teacher. We were talking about being relational with our learners. We were dissecting the notion that no matter the age group of our students, the importance of connecting and establishing a relationship—to be relevant to them—is crucial. She shared a stark example of how out of touch teachers can be. My friend described a particular day during which the school had its scheduled fire-drill practice. It was the morning after a heavy rain. The clouds were still low in the sky, and a light drizzle was falling. (You might ask why anyone would schedule a fire drill during this type of weather but that's a different conversation.) As the fire alarms rang, the kids shuffled out of their various classrooms into the hallway arteries. Some of the nearest exits were down some stairs, and inevitably there was bottlenecking followed by a complete traffic jam. The kids were being herded out into large mud puddles, and they didn't want their precious shoes—their white Adidas, their Jordans—to get muddy. While my friend took notice and tried to usher her students along with compassion in her voice, saying, "We will clean them up, don't worry," another teacher repetitively shouted, "Keep moving, hurry up . . . do not worry about your shoes!"

I thought about this for a long time.

The issue was not really the shoes. No, the shoes were symbolic of so much more for these high schoolers. These shoes represented ownership, a sense of status, a sense of belonging, a sense of P-R-I-D-E. So, in a few seconds, the teacher who was barking orders stripped these learners of all those very personal, meaningful, and uplifting things. This same teacher, while prodding the kids back in the building, would not allow her students to clean their shoes. Meanwhile, my friend got stacks of paper towels, wet them, and set up a shoe-cleaning station in her classroom. I am sure my friend did this as an act of kindness and a show of understanding. She probably didn't even realize that those kids would not have learned anything that morning due to their preoccupation with muddy shoes. For some of those youngsters, those shoes were a special present. For some, they indicated hard work. For others, they represent sacrifice. For still others, they're all of those things. But for all, the shoes are so much more than *just shoes*.

As teachers, we must look beyond contexts such as these to understand our learners and to connect with them. We have to implicitly understand the context of our learners both inside and outside the classroom. This understanding leads to an innate appreciation for them and is another step toward making them feel like they belong. I guarantee the amount of respect my friend earned that day by hosting a shoe-cleaning station, rolling up her sleeves, and helping

While some adults may think shoes are just shoes, for many kids these sneakers may represent a sense of status, belonging, or much more.

remove the mud from her students' shoes went much further than just that moment.

What are your learners' "muddy-shoe moments"? My Littles don't care so much about their shoes. In fact, most days, I am just happy their shoes are on their feet with laces tied. But the analogy is a powerful one. For my Littles, a muddy-shoe moment that I have ignored for the longest time is cutting in line.

We have to implicitly understand the context of our learners both inside and outside the classroom.

Poor grammar aside, it drives me absolutely crazy when my Littles start complaining, "He cutted!" "I was here first!" Recently I asked one Little, "Does it really matter if you are first or second in line? I mean, there are 23 of us. We are all going to get to our destination within about 23 seconds of each other." This is what he said: "Well, it's not really about being first. I was ready. When you said line up, I was ready. I walked to my spot. She ran." For the first time in nearly two decades of teaching, it dawned on me—it is not about being first. Just like it is not about the shoes. The way kids express themselves makes us think it is about the shoes or the place in line. It is often more than that. They just don't know how to express it.

A similar incident occurred on the playground. I saw a Little—let's call him Rory—sitting on the pavement at recess, crying. I asked his teacher what had happened, and she told me that another child reported that Rory had hit her. I was very surprised, as that didn't sound like Rory at all. I called him over and asked for his version of the events. The teacher's jaw hit the ground when Rory very eloquently shared the "trigger" that led to his behavior. He admitted that he had pushed the girl (he demonstrated the action, which, even though it wasn't actually a "hit," was still unacceptable), but even more interesting to me was the reason he did it. Rory explained that the girl was not using the playground equipment according to the rules. As he was trying to go down the slide, she was climbing up the slide, blocking him from going down. Again, Rory's behavior was not acceptable (which I absolutely shared with him!), but instead of automatically doling out punishment to a child, we should try to understand the trigger, even the little sparks, as they do sometimes escalate.

It's not about the shoes. It's not about cutting in line. It's definitely not "bad kids." Teachers, we can trick ourselves into saying things like, "Well, these moments of perceived unfairness teach resilience, to not let little things matter." But . . . really? These instances, seemingly trivial to adults, are not little things to our learners. They are often big things when you look beyond the obvious, ask questions, and truly understand and respect the little things that matter to children.

Moving forward, take a look at the muddy-shoe moments your kids might be experiencing and lean in a little bit. Break down the implicit meaning of the "little moments" and recognize the magnitude of those things in your learners' lives and how we can embrace them and learn from them ourselves.

NUDGE TO RELEVANCE

- **What moments occur in your daily routines that you think are quite little but could reveal something bigger about your learners?**

- **If you aren't aware of these moments, what can you create in your classroom to see these moments more clearly?**

Improve Community

Educators of young students need to have a keen sense of the behaviors and actions of their learners. While young learners are capable and eager, they often turn to the grown-ups in their circle—sometimes explicitly but often subtly—with messages that are inflexible and vulnerable. Teachers of the very young can offer a wider berth for the myriad of behaviors they witness in the classroom, with a focus on building a collective, engaged community. The unspoken understanding of a teacher blossoms into a genuine sense of appreciation of our young learners. This appreciation is the root of our learners' establishing implicit belief in themselves. Being intentional with appreciation means looking at community, relationships within that community, and interactions within those relationships.

The initial approach to establishing a circle of community with young learners is easy. They quickly assimilate and identify as students in a classroom. A community is not a passive entity. It is not derived from a set of rules handed down to its participants. Instead, *community* is derived from an Old English word *gemænscipe*, which means "fellowship, union, common ownership." I use this etymology as another way to utilize vocabulary and engage learners from the beginning.

Each year, I pose these questions to my students: *What is our community? What characteristics do we want our community to be made up of? What is your role in our community?* Of course, being little, their responses parrot one another's: "We are a classroom. We are a school. I am a student. We need to be honest. We need to be kind." Not to say that those answers don't have merit. I acknowledge those answers, but in order to create a community in which everyone develops a sense of belonging, I have to probe further.

Jumping off from this general discussion, I share examples of ideas that will grow a sense of belonging in each learner and will bond us as a learning community. I rely on my Littles to encourage building the concept of community. However, to shape the conversation, I explain the term *community* and its meaning. As their responses above suggest, many young learners have emerging thoughts of the idea of community and the characteristics that identify a community. It is important for young learners to grasp that they belong to different communities, sometimes at the same time. (This always amazes them!) To establish a true sense of belonging, the idea of community needs to be personalized to each classroom and to each learner. I stress that our school community is a place where we live in learning. I emphasize that our classroom is a community built on friendship. We have shared interests, attitudes, and goals. Throughout the conversation, I ask my Littles questions that encourage them to form their individual concepts of community and see the commonalities among peers.

- *What is your favorite thing to learn about at school?*
- *What do you hope to learn this year in our classroom?*
- *What activities do you enjoy outside of school?*
- *What things worry you about learning?*
- *What happens when learning is challenging for you?*
- *What makes you happy?*

Using their responses, I explicitly share that our classroom community is a positive, thinking, problem-solving, and kind community. For example, I might say, "Wow! It sounds like we all have moments that make us happy. We need to remember those moments and what that feels like when we are learning." Or, "Goodness, can you believe we all have things that are challenging for us? Even though what we find difficult is different, we have the same feelings. That is important as we build our community this year."

Teaching is equal parts imagination, determination, inspiration, and animation. You must shape your own questions with intention so that the community you build with your learners is personal to your teaching and learning context. After allowing them the space to think and talk about the notion of belonging in our classroom, I then pose the questions that shape the enduring ideals I want my Littles to be exposed to, reflect on, and grow throughout the school year. We consider the following:

- *How can we be persistent?*
- *How can we be reflective?*
- *How can we be joyful?*
- *How can we be open-minded?*

As a class, we consider and discuss the qualities we want our classroom community to have.

Every year their responses solidify my belief that building relevance through establishing a sense of belonging is truly more about intent than it is about content. My intent, from our discussion, is to set the tone in our classroom community, no matter the content. I expect there to be an intentional stance of developing learners who are persistent, reflective, joyful, and open-minded. How do I know my Littles can grasp such lofty, abstract ideas? In all transparency, I don't know. I hope. It's a journey.

Table graffiti by one of my Littles shows that they're contemplating what it means to be part of our community.

However, when I'm closing down my classroom at the end of the day and notice the word *open-minded* scrawled on a table edge, I know that something is starting to connect, and I will celebrate this table graffiti every single day. It's curious, my learners' responses to such lofty ideas. I am not certain that many adults could answer the prompts with such perceptive ideas. Here are samples of what my six- and seven-year-olds have shared regarding their belonging in our community:

- "I will be persistent by trying."
- "I will be reflective by saying I need help."
- "I will be joyful by being positive."
- "I will be open-minded by listening to other people and not talking."

Once we define our learning community for the year and our personal role in it, we take the time to recognize commonalities and those unfamiliar traits that are part of our community. Recognizing similarities and differences among each member of the community further strengthens the characteristics that bind us and encourages a curiosity to discover characteristics that are different. To do this in a concrete fashion, I use many opportunities for my Littles to explore their diversity and their sameness. We begin with "I Like Myself" bags. I have let go of the mystery bags and boxes from previous years that emphasized hobbies and artifacts and the "what." Instead, I focus now on the characteristics of *who* my children are versus *what* they are. We create a social-emotional shift when we ask children *who* they want to be when they grow up versus *what* they want to be. This subtle, yet intentional shift in thinking builds capacity in our learners to believe that who they are is important and who they want to be is within their reach.

Using a paper bag and the mentor text *I Like Myself!*, by Karen Beaumont, Littles explore how they think people perceive them. (See page 101 for the complete lesson.) They use written words or illustrations and place these on the outside of the bag. Then, for a more introspective look at themselves, they reflect on the things they wish people saw in them— the things they really like about themselves that might be hidden. On small cards, they write down these thoughts and then place the cards inside the bag. I invite my Littles to share. Always, as their teacher,

I peek inside the bags. It can be equally heartwarming and heart-wrenching to see what my Littles wish people knew about them. This activity provides me with a lens to help me understand them better. The last part of this exercise is finding a place in the classroom where the bags can be accessible. Throughout the year, peers add to the bags. When a learner notices something to celebrate in a friend, he or she writes it on a note card and puts it inside that child's bag. Periodically we investigate the contents of our bags. It is pure joy when a Little realizes that a peer recognized what he or she thought was not seen.

"I Like Myself" bags invite children to reflect on how they think people see them and what they wish people knew about them.

Teachers must support young learners in their quest to belong by helping them identify their circle of community and how they interact and belong inside it. The interactions between learners and teacher, and learners and learners are the threads of relevant relationships. In fact, they are more than threads; they are the ties that bind relevance within a learning community.

Improve Relationships

It is not a controversial thought that relationships matter in classrooms. This is the mantra of educators. Unfortunately, this notion is often drowned out by demands of standards, curricula, and mandated assessments. We cannot forgo these requirements. However, they are not the relevant fibers of learning. They are the "must dos," not the ever-joyful "can dos" in education. If we focus on the "can dos," or the intent of educating, then the "must dos," or the content of educating, fall into place.

According to the National Scientific Council on the Developing Child (2004), "young children experience their world as an environment of relationships, and these relationships affect virtually all aspects of their development—intellectual, social, emotional, physical, behavioral, and moral" (p. 1). Classrooms become predictable places in which young learners can establish relationships. To appreciate relationships, teachers must identify what a relationship with learners looks like. Too often, teachers mistake social engagement for a relationship. While social engagement is a stepping-stone for building rapport with our learners, establishing a relationship is so much more than that. Relationships must be relevant. Teachers who craft relevant relationships use a lens of empathy. Relationships with learners are personal. They are centered on learners' curiosities. Relationships are built on learners' pursuits. They are sustained through addressing personal strengths and weaknesses. They are better served through teachable moments than contrived lessons that lack intent. Relationships forge appreciation for one another. Below are some relevant, teachable moments that help build relationships.

Names Learn your learners' names immediately and use them often. It is challenging to establish a relationship with someone when you do not know his or her name. Using learners' names is a true sign of "I see you. I recognize you. I appreciate you." Feel free to ask a learner how to pronounce his or her name. Look up the etymology of names. Appreciate names in the classroom.

Show-and-Tell This is one of those activities that, in today's classrooms, has seemingly gone the way of the wagon. With intentionality, however, there is an argument for doing show-and-tell as it allows us a glimpse into our learners' lives. Show-and-tell is a platform to learn more about our learners and for them to learn more about one another. At the most basic level, it is a practice that involves speaking, listening, and asking. The show-and-tell experience should be inclusive and not be a stressor for families. Put the responsibility for the task on young learners. Consider these options as you commit to an opportunity for your learners to show and tell.

- Have a grab bag of relevant mystery items and allow learners to extemporaneously speak about an object.
- Establish a theme for what learners share each week. For example, show and tell your favorite word, your favorite dance move, color, number, and so on.
- Turn show-and-tell into a "show-and-don't-tell." Have learners sketch or illustrate their object.
- Cover a show-and-tell item and invite the learner's peers to ask probing questions about the item.

Displaying Children's Work Look around a school's hallways and the displays of learners' work. Many times, what we observe are exemplary samples of a task. Teachers show off the best of the best. When we think about it, this is the opposite of the message we should be sending to our learners. In our continued effort to move away from one-size-fits-all teaching and learning, we also should consider moving away from one-size-fits-all displays of children's work. Choose an artifact that represents failure and then learning. Choose an artifact that is almost there. Choose an artifact that can serve as commentary for next steps. Display samples of exemplars when it is pertinent, but also display authentic learning that values processes. I purchase an inexpensive frame each year and border it with the words "You've Been Framed." My Littles look forward to the work that will be displayed and our conversation about its merit. A colleague has created a timeline on the classroom wall and displays one or two samples or stories or recaps of her students' learning each month. On larger projects, I focus on the process. My displays are messy. Isn't learning messy? The display builds as the learning builds. As our teaching transforms to focus on relevance, so should our expressions of the learning.

> *Display samples of exemplars when it is pertinent, but also display authentic learning that values processes.*

Routines and Rituals Young learners thrive on procedures and formalities in the classroom. Do not confuse this approach with rigidity and conformity. I challenge you to hand over the control to your learners. Create class expectations together. Start the year off by asking, "What do you expect of me?" Be daring. Invite your learners to help prepare the learning space. I know. I spent decades matching every accessory, every curtain, every nameplate—until I stopped. The first year my learners walked into a classroom in complete organized chaos and I handed them a piece of paper and said, "Design our learning space this year," it made such an impact. While I still did some strategic designing, I gave my young learners the opportunity to own the space they inhabited. Their expectations were immediately high.

Classroom responsibilities or jobs is another area teachers use to establish routine and rituals. I don't disagree that jobs can create a sense of belonging. They support a sense of community, but are they truly relevant? Are jobs implemented so teachers can control the order in a classroom, or are jobs implemented in a way that involves everyone taking an active role in moderating behavior and learning? Take, for example, real life. We are not assigned to be first in line or last in line. Instead, we have learned social cues and use them. We have learned how to wait our turn. We don't raise our hand when we want to speak to someone; we listen first, we lean on the nuances of conversation, and we know when it's time to share our thinking. We apologize if we interrupt someone. I am certain what I am suggesting is challenging for some to read, and it does not happen all at once. But, if we are truly being relevant with our learners and focusing on the intent of everything we do in our classrooms through implicit understanding while building relationships, then we must reflect on rituals and routines. Change them up and give some of the stringent rules a new birth.

*

With a refreshed approach to appreciating relationships, learners construct an interdependent or mutually dependent approach to learning. Relationships are about learning. Through them, we learn about others, we learn from others, and we learn with others.

Relationships are the underpinning to a strong classroom community and must be established and valued by the teacher. Included in this interdependent, community-driven approach to relationship building is the incentive for the teacher to address the spontaneity of a positive, inclusive community. In our classrooms, we need to embrace interdependence, warm demands, belief, trust, and failure.

Improve Learners' Interdependence

Classrooms that advance young learners who think and do things for themselves with a proactive stance value community. However, with the notion of independence, there also needs to be a shift to interdependence, or leaning on one another. One of the easiest ways to foster this belief is to establish a classroom community.

An Expert Wall provides an opportunity for further promoting community. It is also a natural place to post jobs and responsibilities. Instead of exerting teacher control on what children should be leading, an Expert Wall allows for learner reflection and voice. In any new classroom, there is an immediate, natural recognition of strengths and weaknesses among learners. As teachers, we witness them, but peers also see these traits in one another. The Expert Wall capitalizes on how young learners see themselves and how they see their classmates.

An Expert Wall helps young learners recognize and acknowledge their strengths, which peers can utilize.

Set up time during a morning meeting for a brainstorming session. Ask your learners the following:

- *What areas of our classroom need attention every day?* (Responses may include: supplies, classroom pets, learning space organization, lunch count, and so on. Personalize this to your classroom and guide your learners along the conversation.)

- *What areas of learning are sometimes difficult?* (Responses may include: math, reading, technology, and so on.)

Then encourage your learners to think about their belonging inside the classroom. Ask:

- *What classroom organization talents do you have that can help your peers?*

- *What learning or academic talents do you have that can help your peers?*

- *Can you think of anything else that gives you ownership in this classroom that will help all of us to have a great year together?*

Feel free to expand on this idea. You can create a job application that invites learners to reflect on and respond to personalized questions. Or, if you're like me, you can handle this same task in an open conversation.

I use note cards and sticky notes all the time to organize, show, and share thinking. Littles decide where their strengths are, and I don't challenge that. Isn't it funny how Littles often don't see the challenges we see and think they are famously strong at every single task? But that's okay. The intent (there we go again!) is to develop interdependence. If a Little says he is great at technology, and the first time someone needs help in technology and the Little can't deliver, some very authentic conversation and learning takes place. The broader perspective is that through this experience young learners recognize their individual, valued strengths, which are utilized and celebrated by every learning community member.

My Expert Wall display is merely framed paper with headings that change, depending on my classroom needs. The experts change, too. While I don't limit how many things a Little can be an expert on, I suggest to them that because they will be responsible for the work the expert needs to accomplish, they should focus on one or two expert gifts. It is remarkable to see the levels of confident independence and interdependence grow and transform the classroom community. The wall remains all year and continues to change, depending on the needs of our classroom and the growth of learners. When students identify themselves with a new expertise, they can move their name to another frame.

The wall is a big deal at the very beginning of the school year, but it swiftly becomes a part of the classroom culture. For example, when Aidan has trouble organizing his notebook, he looks at the wall and sees that Hope is a master organizer and asks her for help. When at the end of a day the classroom looks well loved and needs a little TLC, Matthew, the expert tidier, gets to work. Of course, there are times when the teacher must facilitate this. When little eyes peer at me and say, "I don't understand . . . ," I can glance at the wall and say, "Did you ask Silas for help? He's a mathematician!" Poignantly, as the weeks pass, Littles rely less and less on me and more and more on one another in significant ways that matter.

Improve on Making Warm Demands

Many years ago, I attended an Extra Yard for Teachers event and was introduced to the idea of being a "warm demander." It was a moment of wonder for me. As teachers, we are often asked, "How do you manage your classroom?" Over two decades, this question has always stumped me. Not the question itself, but the answer. There are so many classroom-management trade materials on the market. There are so many philosophies we can try in a classroom. Year after year, it seemed my classroom management became a blend of so many different ideas. Then, I heard the phrase "warm demander." It truly was a moment of revelation for me. While I believe relationships with children are the cornerstone of any classroom-management approach, I also believe being a warm demander is the support beam to the relationship structure with children.

Warm demanders encourage students to establish for themselves a sense of independence, a sense of control, and, most importantly, a sense of belief. Warm demanders do not breed conformity. Instead, being a warm demander breaks down equity barriers. Being a warm demander means setting lofty expectations for all learners. Warm demanders hold learners accountable for mistakes in a firm but loving way. It is not nitpicking, punishment, or unnatural consequences, especially for those learners who don't meet your expectations. Instead, a warm, demanding relationship fosters regulation and routine and direction and discipline. Warm demands illustrate that learning is hard work and that the effort through learning ultimately leads to success. It is critical to establish nonnegotiable beliefs in the classroom, such as: "struggle matters," "failure is a celebration of learning," and "thinking is heavy lifting." My Littles recognize me as a warm demander because of my tone and my intentional words. Every single day young learners deserve a teacher whose stance says, "I believe in you, I have big love for you, and I trust you." With this established, a teacher's message becomes one of belief and trust that young learners echo.

> *Being a warm demander means setting lofty expectations for all learners.*

Improve Your Belief

Do you believe in your learners? By default, do you look for the cracks, no matter how small, that cause struggle, or do you flip the script and look at the corners that connect and the openings that are filled? It is easy to say we believe in our students. It is more challenging to do the work that sustains our belief in them. To maintain a belief in our learners, we must address equity, we must address diversity, and we must stop encouraging the bar to be set high. When we consider the bar being set high, it creates constriction. Rather, we must find camaraderie in not having a bar at all and realizing that if we believe in our learners through our words, our actions, and our intentional relationship building, the bar dissolves for them, too. They simply rise from a belly-driven belief they have in themselves because of the trust we have enveloped them in.

Improve Trust

Druckerman (2012) relates an example of French parenting that translates well into classrooms that want to implicitly build trust. In France, parents are typically strict about things that matter. They create and express boundaries but openly trust children to be independent within the limitations set. In short, children are granted the autonomy to make mistakes and learn from them. This concept holds true in classrooms that are focused on building relationships. I quibble with the word *boundary* and prefer the term *expectations*, or at the least, suggest movable or flexible boundaries. These expectations do not need to rely on complete, explicit "sharing of the rules." Instead, we create expectations collaboratively, and they continue to gain importance through assimilation within the classroom. If we set boundaries and are inflexible with them, we are not relying on the relevant matters that shape our learners.

Improve With Failure

Create a space where your learners see failure as important. Sara Blakely, founder of Spanx, often shares an anecdote about her father. Weekly, at the dinner table, Blakely's father would ask, "What did you fail at this week?" Candidly, Blakely shares that if she or her brother had nothing to share, their father had an air of disappointment. He believed that failure was important in creating and becoming.

In classrooms, we need to capitalize on failure. If we nudge young learners to reflect daily on moments of failure and, more importantly, what they gleaned from the flop, they understand that failing is learning. Human brains must have a level of disequilibrium before meaning is created. To illustrate this for young learners, have them stand up. After a moment, ask them to stand on one foot and try to stay balanced. For those who have a good sense of balance, have them close their eyes and remain balanced. Explain that this is like their brain trying to learn something. Ask children to describe how it feels. Expect comments such as "weird and wobbly" and "not straight" and "awful." Explain that this is how learning should feel.

Failure is uncomfortable, especially for young learners. Contrive tasks that force mistakes. Establish a place of ambiguity with tasks. For example, ask hazy questions in which a correct answer could be proven incorrect. Uncertainty for young learners can elicit the same discomfort that failure does.

We all make mistakes. If you misspell a word or hand out a task that happens to have a typographical error or if you accidentally call a student by the wrong name, capitalize on your mistake with your young learners. Call out the mistake and briefly explain how it made you feel—from embarrassment to silliness to worry. Then emphasize what you learned from the mistake and stress that you are still the same person you were before making the mistake. Celebrating mistakes as part of learning has a welcome place in my classroom. We catalog these mistakes in my "Grown-Up's Oops Book." It used to be called the "Teacher's Oops Book" until one afternoon the principal announced the wrong date on the intercom. Immediately, my Littles recognized the mistake and asked for it to be included in the book.

Seeing failure as a positive step toward learning promotes a growth mindset.

The acronym First Attempt in Learning (FAIL) is a kitschy way to think about failure. Can your learners think of another acronym to embrace failure and the emotional and cognitive steps we need to take to move forward? Seeing failure as a positive step toward learning promotes a growth mindset. Our society is so focused on success that we often miss the reflective nature that failing can prompt. As we journey through our year together, the idea of making mistakes means learning is commonplace. The "Oops Book" becomes an artifact of reflection, and young learners begin to identify failure as a natural and accepted part of their learning. While the emotions that surround failure can remain challenging for Littles, as they learn to embrace it, they become better positioned to identify how they could do better, what improvements they can make, and what steps they can take to succeed. In short, failure is the gateway to gaining a strong belief in oneself.

FIVE

Tackle Emotionality
Life Is Lumpy

Have you ever had a student cry? Perhaps something was too difficult for him, or maybe she wasn't being heard, taken seriously, or understood . . . you get the picture. Robert Fulghum shared, "Life is lumpy." Teaching this to Littles is important when it comes to helping them understand relevant responses to many of life's events. Fulghum further explains that there are lumps in your oatmeal, lumps in your throat, and lumps in your breast*; each metaphor helps us identify and tackle life's challenges. I use this analogy with my Littles.

When things go sideways or your Littles feel frustrated, share relevant responses. To a six-year-old, it may be very relevant for him or her to burst into tears. Most things that occur in a classroom are oatmeal lumps. I encourage my Littles to take out their imaginary wooden spoon and stir and stir until the lump goes away. Explain that lumpy oatmeal isn't the best, but it's also not the end of the world. Share examples of lumpy-oatmeal moments, such as forgetting an assignment, not feeling part of a collaborative group, struggling with a new concept, or simply being too tired that day. To continue with the analogy, discuss a lump in your throat. Sometimes when we feel like we are going to cry, our eyes fill up

---

* For some young learners, sadly, a lump in the breast can be a very relevant idea. It is important to know your students and their families and how a conversation such as this could be triggering. You can modify this description as a lump on your body, as in a physical ailment or injury. It is a delicate conversation but an important one to guide young learners on how to discern acceptable and necessary emotional responses over those that are merely emotional reactions.

and we feel the need to swallow hard. Usually, our lump-in-the-throat moments come from a place of strong emotion—and not a nice one at that. Discuss how sometimes it is okay to cry; but unless we can share words behind the emotion, it might be better to swallow hard, blink back the tears, and move forward. Lastly, of course, we discuss a lump in your breast. These "lumpy moments," as I refer to them, are the dire moments that are life-changing. While I share that we are always allowed a reaction, it is during these lumpy moments when we likely need help and support to get through them. It's a strong analogy for Littles, but they get it.

Teaching children social-emotional skills is an important step in promoting positive behaviors.

Soon, you will observe relevant reactions to things. This changes the interactions and allows for social discourse, promotes listening, and allows for leaning in. In short, it creates a strong, risk-free, supportive environment—a cornerstone of creating a relevant classroom.

NUDGE TO RELEVANCE

- How can you support social discourse in your classroom?
- Besides stopping the conversation when social discourse doesn't go as expected, what else can you do?

Social-Emotional Confidence

Social-emotional learning is fundamental for young learners. Social-emotional learning promotes academic achievement and strong, positive behaviors (Dusenbury & Weissberg, 2017). The hearts of our young learners are intricate, so meeting their emotional needs becomes more involved. Strategically, teachers can tackle emotionality through an affective lens, with a cognitive flourish. If I asked you to list the soft skills, learning ideas, or values that are important to young learners, you would have a lengthy list. However, as with most learning, even social-emotional learning needs to be addressed individually. Tending to the social-emotional needs of young learners requires endurance. When it comes to building social-emotional confidence in young learners, teachers often find themselves on a hamster wheel.

Start with your learners. Ask them: *What important skills do we need to complete this specific task? What characteristic do you need to lean on to learn this material? How are you going to finish this task when you are stuck? What are you going to do when you get the answer wrong?* They may be little, but they know intuitively. If they speak the words, then we should assume their ideas are important to them, and we need to find a place in their learning to support it.

While many districts employ a social-emotional learning curriculum, tackling emotionality is on-the-job training. Reading a picture book about a child who blurts out will not resonate with children who do not blurt out or who are not at the developmental stage to recognize themselves in the story. However, as we lean in and begin to look for cues in our learners, we can build a repertoire of strategies for responding to the emotions of our young learners. When we are intentional with how we handle young learners' emotionality, we purposefully communicate self-regulation. This leads to social-emotional confidence. Learners should be allowed to have emotional, visceral reactions to certain contexts. However, I would argue that few of the reactions we sometimes see actually relate to what's happening in our classrooms. Even if your district or your role in a classroom supports a social-emotional curriculum, there are relevant matters we can tackle with an assured, trusting approach each day with our learners.

Tackle Predictability

Consider the expectedness of your learning environment. Creating a predictable schedule with predictable expectations does not mean being inflexible and rigid. In fact, within creating a predictable environment, we need to consider flexibility and creativity. Predictability just means that within the framework of a learner's day, there is a sameness that is likely. Observe your learners on a day when school starts late or a fire drill interrupts your lesson. These normal but unanticipated events unnerve them. "Children who are provided with a predictable schedule and secure environment are more likely to feel confident about exploring their world. . . . Through these explorations, children strengthen their connections to the people and environment around them" (Klein, 2002). Unavoidable things happen in classrooms, just as they do in life. However, the comfort of predictable patterns allows learners to strengthen their autonomy in those areas and manage the unexpected moments with confidence when they do arise. The predictable nature of classroom learning is an invitation to stability, both physical and emotional.

Tackle Affective Learning

Benjamin Bloom (1956) established a theory of three learning domains or taxonomies that complement a student's learning skills: cognitive learning (thinking), psychomotor learning (doing), and affective learning (feeling).

The affective domain deals with behavior and feelings and how they are managed. It is this domain that supports emotionality with young learners. I share with my Littles as I share with you: "This is the heart stuff. This is the stuff that makes you a really cool human. This is the stuff that no matter who you become in the world, you will be ready for challenges and celebrations." Yet, it is so much more than "stuff."

Affective learning bridges culture. Affective learning is equitable. Affective learning allows for our learners to engage in personalized reflection. It allows for our learners to recognize human frailties. Affective learning is a bridge to cognition. When we can foster an environment that enables young learners to tackle their emotionality, they establish a keen self-awareness. The position of affective learning or social-emotional learning in a classroom is not to quash behaviors or manipulate learners to stop their emotions. Instead, affective learning provides a foundation for young learners as they continue to grow in acceptance of and confidence about their abilities. Incorporating the affective needs of our learners throughout our curriculum sends a message of trust and belief.

Social-emotional learning is based on five competencies: self-awareness, self-management, decision making, social awareness, and relationship skills (Collaborative for Academic, Social, and Emotional Learning, 2012). Addressing the affective domain is not segregated into these competencies. Instead, teachers need to see emotionality in young learners as an opportunity to build relevance with them. It would be nice if the social-emotional needs of our learners were predictable and always fit into the lesson plan for the day; however, that is not realistic. With that in mind, there are ways we can address social-emotional needs, regardless of the curriculum. This approach lies firmly in exposing young learners to the arts and to literature, sometimes in tandem.

Integrating the Arts

Throughout history, art has proved to be an instrument of emotions. Silverstein and Layne (2010) define *arts integration* as "an approach to teaching in which students construct and demonstrate understanding through an art form. Students engage in a creative process, which connects an art form and another subject area and meets evolving objectives in both" (p. 1). A growing body of research suggests that integrating the arts in classrooms supports many facets of a learner's noncognitive function, including social-emotional prowess (Steel, 2016). The arts, with their attention on expression, feelings, and awareness, are a perfect place for young learners to explore their own emotions— how to identify and process them. The arts provide a backdrop to social-emotional learning that is authentic and connective. There are innumerable ways you can integrate the arts into your classroom. Here are a few activities to consider.

Puppetry Using puppetry allows for the displacement of emotions and a creative space to explore emotions in different ways. Some of your most quiet, introverted, unsure learners can use puppetry as a representation of themselves. Learners can make their own puppet creations or use premade puppets. You will witness the discovery of personal voice if you invite learners to share reflections, thoughts, and ideas through a puppet's actions and voice. At the beginning of the school year, my Littles make puppets to represent themselves. We spend a little time learning about the author Ashley Bryan and his penchant for making puppets out of anything. Littles take to the task and create unique puppets out of repurposed materials, clay, or wooden spoons. The puppets live in our classroom, and learners use them in various contexts throughout the year.

A shy learner may find it easier to express herself through a puppet.

Each year, I introduce a mascot in the form of a puppet. In recent years, a large stuffed llama has occupied a special place in our classroom. He sits, sometimes dressed in accessories the Littles create, and he simply listens. When an individual or group is having difficulties with an emotion, they "save the drama for the llama" and engage in a conversation with him. It is fascinating to watch a Little speak to him and respond as him. Or, if a group needs to compromise, one of the Littles may take on the voice of the llama and help problem-solve. The joyful part is that as their teacher, I hear intent that has derived from implicit learning in our classroom. Alternately, Littles can write the llama a letter in his "Llama-Llove Journal" and wait for his response. If anything, it is an engaging place where Littles can share their issues and process them independently in a personal space without a teacher navigating the context for them.

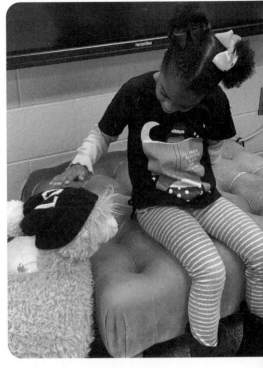

We have a llama that "listens" to any learner who needs to talk through a problem.

Pantomime Young learners need to explore nonverbal communication. Animals, for example, do not use words to communicate, yet we often understand what our pets need by their sounds or movements. This is a comfortable starting place to illustrate to young learners how we can understand messages without words. Stress the importance of learning to listen with your eyes and your heart. We can learn empathy if we open our eyes and read nonverbal messages and allow those messages to affect our hearts. Pantomime is an expressive tool that focuses on facial expressions and body movement. While lessons that produce pantomime expression are contrived, the experience helps young learners capture social cues and nuances of nonverbal messages. It is another piece to understanding one's own emotions and regulating them. Simply ask learners: *Without words, can you show me how you feel?* Or model the same and ask learners what messages they can read from your posture or your face. Ironically, the skill of reading nonverbal messages has been more prominently needed as teachers and learners were often masked during the COVID-19 pandemic of 2020–21.

Visual Arts Expression Historically, images have been used to tell culturally relevant stories, and our current world is rich in images. Use visual arts as an opportunity for young learners to explore emotions. "A picture is worth a thousand words" may be cliché, but it is also true. Merely sharing an image with young learners prompts an emotional response. Selecting intentional, relevant images is a lesson hook that compels young learners to see attitudes and behaviors within the image.

Much could be written on the impact that visual arts have on a young learner's emotional regulation and its expression. Through various media, visual arts provide a creative outlet for the very same competencies that social-emotional learning curriculum demands. From drawing a self-portrait to responding to a prompt based on a mentor text to creating a more elaborate project, such activities provide a consistent and powerful place for emotional reflection and growth to be represented visually.

Self-portraits give valuable insight into how learners see themselves.

Linking Literature

Literature is another powerful tool for addressing social-emotional needs. Many picture books examine myriad social-emotional traits. Be intentional when choosing literature for your class. If your learners as a group do not struggle with a specific characteristic presented in a story, the purpose is lost. While many lessons can be derived from a picture book, simply reading a story and drawing out the social-emotional strengths or weaknesses of a character allows for young learners to place themselves in the story. "There is evidence that our brains treat interactions between fictional characters similarly to real-life social experiences" (Pinto, 2019). Thus, rich picture books that contain topics important to human social and emotional life are prime for our classrooms.

Stories in picture books create an awareness for young children as characters display ways to handle challenges, creative problem solving, and embracing differences (Roberts & Crawford, 2008). Not surprisingly, frequent readers are better able to empathize with others and see the world from different perspectives (Paul, 2012). The Relevant Lessons in Chapter 10 are a nod to my own love of literature. My Littles expect and celebrate that most of my lessons integrate literature. In fact, if you were to ask them how I like to share books, you would hear a chorus of, "Cover to cover!" I read every part of a picture book with them and revel in the details. *Who might this person on the dedication line be? What were the author's emotions when she wrote this book? Why did the illustrator choose this color to represent this page? How old is this text if the copyright date is 1967? Where is Philadelphia?* While these questions do not jibe with social-emotional learning, they stress the importance of mining picture books for every ounce of relative meaning you can muster.

I would be remiss if I gave the impression that simply integrating arts and sharing beautifully crafted literature with your learners will quash the need to address other drastic behaviors. We must remember, our learners are young. While often predictable, they also exhibit unforeseen behaviors that need more immediacy than what may have previously been suggested. Exposing young learners to the arts and literature builds social-emotional awareness and stamina. The lessons and morals learned from them do much to intercept unwanted behaviors, but sometimes we still have to address behavior as a separate entity.

Tackle Behavior

It is hard to be little. The often asynchronous development of little brains and little hearts sometimes makes things go a bit haywire for our young learners. They don't understand, and as their teachers, we can only marvel. Many, many years ago, I went through an intensive Love and Logic Education training. It was part of my school's professional learning for the year as we tried to establish some consistency with behavior management. While I believe the best behavior management plan is made up of all the big and small ideas in this book, my personal study of and interest in *Teaching With Love and Logic* (Fay & Funk, 1995) shaped my approach to building a classroom community. The principles in that book are enduring, but there was one idea I learned in my Love and Logic training that has never left my teaching toolbox. The gist of this tool is to create a one-liner that you can consistently use to deflect a poor behavior choice.

Giving learners space to reflect on their conduct gives them space to own their behavior.

A one-liner is simply a comment or a phrase that gives learners the space to think. I am not sure why this has made the biggest impact with my most difficult learners, but it has. Every year my one-liner changes, depending on my class. Sometimes, I have a repertoire of one-liners that I use on an individual basis. It defuses what could be a combative situation.

Among my favorites:

It is so hard to be little, I agree.
Goodness, I'm not sure what I think about that.
You know, as your teacher, I care about you too much
*   to argue about this.*
You know what? I'm going to think about it for a bit.

I employ these one-liners when my learners challenge what is happening in the classroom. I use a one-liner when a young learner doesn't meet a behavioral expectation in our classroom. I approach the statement with compassion and empathy. When I initially respond to a poor behavior with a one-liner, my Littles are often taken aback. They don't really know what to say. Perhaps young learners are used to punishment. Or perhaps this approach really does give them pause for thought. Either way, it's effective. Think of a one-liner you can use with your young learners.

It would be grand to think that a one-liner is all it takes to avoid even the worst outbursts. I'm much more realistic than that. However, because teachers need to curate a space of learning, we need to tread carefully when it comes to addressing behaviors. There are certain behaviors that demand full, direct attention with natural consequences. But consider tackling behavior with empathy and compassion. Discover the antecedent to the behavior. Remember, these learners are but little and are just exploring ideals.

Tackle Ideals That Are Important in Your Classroom Community

For my Littles, every year there are naturally relevant ideals that become established in my classroom. Sometimes they derive from the greater world—things happening in our society that offer an opportunity to teach values. Other times, ideals result from a significant experience in our classroom. Now and then, I simply use my understanding of what principles young learners need to carry with them to establish a core confidence in themselves. After many years, a theme has evolved. Principles of positivity, empathy, fairness, failure, resilience, and passion have become the important social-emotional attitudes we address in my classroom. While these traits hold specific value, their intent is far-reaching. They become a consistent refrain in everything my Littles do. While these beliefs may differ from your classroom context, I invite you to consider them and why they matter.

Positivity

There is an upside to even the most negative situations; we just have to be open to the learning and recognize the power of positive thinking. I want my learners to be genuine with their emotions. Humans are allowed a reaction, and sometimes it is hard to see the silver lining when a situation feels dark. I share a lesson about the term *silver lining* with my Littles. We look at clouds that have that glow and discuss how the term was derived. (The term *silver lining* can be traced back to a 1634 poem by John Milton in which he refers to a dark cloud with a halo or sliver of sun or moonlight around its edges. This literary phrase became part of idiomatic expression in literature and ultimately found its way into popular expression.)

After we investigate images of real clouds illustrating this phenomenon, I invite young learners to create an "Upside Journal." This journal is a receptacle for moments of positivity that can be found in an unlikely experience or thought. I stress that there is learning in all contexts, which, in and of itself, is the upside. I share theme music from decades ago to more-current pop favorites that connect to being happy, letting things go, feeling good, and so on. While the music plays, my Littles draw or write about an experience that didn't go the way they thought

An Upside Journal provides a space for Littles to reflect on the "upside" of an experience that didn't go their way.

it should and the upside to the situation. These journals take on a life of their own. Some Littles title them "Perspective Journals," while others choose "Silver Lining Journals," but they are all filled with examples of young learners' connecting real-life disappointments, worries, and problems to something positive. It creates a mind-shift, and as a teacher you begin to see roadblocks for learners disappear. You begin to sense a culture shift in the classroom in which Littles start to consistently believe in what they can do, no matter the outcome.

Empathy

One of the more challenging values to teach is empathy. While an understanding of empathy creates compassion in our classroom community, I struggle with whether empathy is an innate trait that some people possess while others do not and whether empathy can truly be taught. I believe sympathy is a concrete idea; simply put, it's "I feel sorry for you." Empathy is that abstract idea of "I feel sorry *with* you." General psychological research asserts that empathy can be taught. Given that Littles sometimes don't even seem to understand their own emotions, it seems an immense task to expect them to understand and feel someone else's emotions. Empathy is important, even if young learners only get to the level of understanding another's perspective. Empathy allows a view of others from diverse backgrounds. Empathy can expand Littles' exposure to the world. Empathy builds open-mindedness and harmony among peers.

As you tackle empathy, anchor your lessons with images. Share photographs of people or animals in hypothetical emotional situations and solicit responses from learners about what the person or animal may be feeling. Use picture books to explore empathy. Here are some of my favorites for developing empathy in the classroom:

- *One*, by Kathryn Otoshi
- *Hey, Little Ant*, by Phillip and Hannah Hoose
- *I'm Here*, by Peter H. Reynolds
- *The Invisible Boy*, by Trudy Ludwig
- *Leonardo, the Terrible Monster*, by Mo Willems

Fairness

My Littles love to inform me about every little unfair act that happens in our classroom community. Young learners are righteous in their approach to fairness. We must teach young learners that "fair" does not mean "equal." Teaching fairness predisposes young learners to see things from a less egocentric perspective and consider others' point of view. Grasping the concept of fairness allows young learners to rebound from disappointment. Fairness also provides the impetus for young learners to understand negotiation and compromise. Young learners look at fairness with an incomplete understanding.

I explain the important idea of fairness through a quirky but concrete demonstration with treats. (I use Skittles for this demonstration, but feel free to use any coveted, low-cost, bite-size treats, such as popcorn or pretzels.) I ask for two volunteers. Next, I share that I have 10 treats to share with the volunteers. Some Littles begin to grumble, and I begin to hear whispers of, "Hey, that's not fair." As I distribute the treats, I explain that one friend is going to get six treats while the other friend is going to get four. The Littles who receive the treats are a little bit unsure. I encourage them to eat the treats, and then I ask, "Was that fair?" Immediately I hear groaned responses, and most of the class settles on the belief that it was not fair because one friend got more treats than the other. I use this opportunity to explain that it is fair; it is just not equal. I share my perspective that two friends started with zero treats and they each ended up with some treats. I then wait for the argument that it isn't fair because everyone else in the class didn't get any treats. When that argument comes, I reiterate: It is fair, it just isn't equal. This demonstration makes a point, and to emphasize it even more, I give every learner two treats at the end of the lesson. That is what it takes for them to agree that there is some fairness in that.

Failure

Earlier, I spoke to the importance of acknowledging and celebrating failure and the learning that we derive from failure. Introduce young learners to important people from a historical and biographical perspective to expose them to the disappointments, challenges, failures, and ultimate successes experienced by these figures. Seek out historical figures embedded in learning standards and examine their experiences for ones that illustrate failure. Tune into young learners' pop-culture references and explore the challenges and failures of celebrities.

Connecting to real-life examples of failure is influential on young learners. There are many familiar, famous faces who exemplify failure equaling success. Take, for example, Babe Ruth, one of the greatest baseball players of all time. Ruth hit 714 home runs but struck out even more, at 1,330 times. As a young man, Abraham Lincoln opened a general store that failed, yet he became one of the greatest presidents in United States history. Consider Michael Jordan, one of the best basketball players of all time. He didn't make his high school basketball team. Even the Wright brothers crashed seven flying machines while inventing their airplane. Oprah Winfrey, Walt Disney, and many more well-known people illustrate the success that can come from failure. Celebrating failure allows young learners to witness what it means to bounce back when facing adversity.

Resilience

Resilience, the ability to bounce back, is another challenging hurdle young learners need to assimilate into their academic and social experiences in the classroom. Like many of the competencies discussed in this book, being flexible, not sweating the small stuff, and being able to pivot are not easy concepts to express in a concrete manner for young learners.

Teach children to "be like a duck."

Because imagery, animals, and mantras are favorites in my classroom, I explain that being resilient is like letting water roll off a duck's back. While the expression emerged in the 1800s, the imagery is perfect for today's young learners navigating challenging contexts. I share a video of a duck in water, taking a bath. (The science behind this phenomenon is quite fascinating but tangential to the meaning I want my learners to derive from the imagery.) While my Littles watch the video clip, I challenge them to think of themselves as a duck and of the water as all the things that worry, upset, or challenge them. I ask: *What happens to the water on the duck's back?*

They see that it easily rolls off. I then ask: *What would happen if the water did not roll off a duck's back?* Responses include: *The duck would sink* or *It would feel heavy*. You can see the pattern of my questioning because next comes: *What happens if we let our worries, upsets, or challenges pile up on our backs?* Of course, we would feel heavy. "Be Like a Duck" is a common refrain we use to defuse situations in my classroom. While this little piece of information does not keep Littles from feeling frustrated and worried or alleviate the challenges they may face, it does give them an anchor to hold on to when things get prickly.

Another favorite analogy that brings the abstract idea of resilience to terms young learners can embrace is the Super-Ball-versus-egg challenge. I introduce this as a simple lesson in goal-setting. I set up a large bull's-eye target on the floor. We stand around the target and share small goals we are striving for. Each Little shares his or her immediate goal, which does not have to be school-related. After leaning in and listening to their goals, I choose several Littles to illustrate the important part of this lesson. I hand each one a Super Ball and ask them to share their goal. Then I have them aim the Super Ball to try and hit the bull's-eye. Even with fair accuracy, the Super Ball tends to bounce out and miss the bull's-eye. Before I can say anything, undoubtedly the Little herself or a peer will say, "Try again!" If the lesson goes that way, I interject: "Wait, wait, wait. You

Trying to hit a bull's-eye target with a bouncy Super Ball teaches my learners a lesson in resilience.

mean you didn't get it right the first time, and you're going to try again? Interesting." This continues several times. To be clear, this often evolves into a raucous attempt by each Little to hit the mark that represents their goal. Of course, some Littles do hit the bull's-eye, and we celebrate. However, they implicitly understand the idea of being a Super Ball when things don't go right.

Because we want young learners to believe in themselves, we must model our own struggles when the opportunity allows. For this lesson, I share my own immediate goal, choosing something that is sometimes humorous and often relatable. Unbeknownst to my Littles, I have hidden a raw egg in my hand prior to the lesson. When it is my turn to share my goal and try to hit the bull's-eye, I throw the egg. I purposely miss the target and pause. After the laughter subsides, I hear a small whisper, "It's okay. You were close." Empathy on display! However, the point I want to make is that if we act like eggs when we don't meet our goals or when we try something new and fail, we don't get a second chance. Without spelling this out for young learners, they understand. Another common catchphrase I use in the classroom is, "Are you acting like a Super Ball or an egg right now?" To close out the lesson, I provide a chance for each Little to reflect personally on how to be a Super Ball and not an egg to practice resilience.

Passion

Young learners are just discovering what excites them. In much of their lives, grown-ups decide for them what hobbies and interests to engage in. Our classroom is a place where Littles can realize personal aspirations. As I have repeated several times, if they communicate something, it is important to them. This is true when you tap into the zeal of young learners. They have introduced me to so many things I would have never known about. From Minecraft to parkour to indigenous foods to dance moves and jingles, Littles have sparks of delights that we can nurture into passionate learning. There is time in our classroom for exploration of passions. Hopefully, you start to see the tight weaves of relevance, in which one action leads to another action, which leads to another action, much like in the book *If You Give a Mouse a Cookie*, by Laura Numeroff. If we lean in, build relationships, create a space that is understanding of all learners, and tackle their emotionality, the intersection of teacher practice and student mindset of belonging, believing, and becoming are tightly bonded. Ask your learners: *What excites you? What do you wonder about? What are you curious about?* It really is as simple as accepting their developmentally appropriate responses.

Littles have sparks of delight that we can nurture into passionate learning.

Littles love their family, they love their cats and dogs, they love sports, they love their teachers (we hope!). As their teacher, shape their zest for hobbies, projects, and talents into activities that tap into their enthusiasm in a meaningful way. Use their relevant personal pursuits and make them matter.

Years ago, I created a passion project called "The Great So-What?" I invited my young learners to start thinking about things they feel passionate about. As Littles were brainstorming ideas and meeting with me to confer, I found myself repeating, "So what? Why does this matter to you?" It isn't that their ideas were not valid; I just didn't see ideas bursting with *oomph*. Littles' passions often come from a very limited circle of experience; but that doesn't mean their projects can't develop into something bigger. I watched as a young learner whose passion was snakes turn a subject matter (that, to be honest, I found very unexciting) into a project that served hikers in our area. He created a placard to share with hikers on local trails about the snakes native to our area and the safety rules to adhere to when encountering these snakes. Anecdotally, this young learner brought his snake into my classroom the day of our presentations. He skipped into the room with a pillowcase in hand and said, "Can I leave this here for a minute while I go to the library?"

Distracted with getting something ready for the morning, I muttered, "What is it?" He replied with an incredulous tone, "My snake, of course! I'm presenting today, right?" That young learner rode on the bus with his snake in a pillowcase all the way to school!

That comical incident aside, the entire learning process was a turning point for me as a teacher. I have always enjoyed passionate experiences and worked to create events to breed passion in my learners. I assumed my learners would embrace my passions and appreciate them. I think they do, but teachers must help learners mine the "so what" so they can understand that their own passions are more expansive than they appear on the surface. Aside from inviting young learners to share what excites them, consider the following as you guide them to explore excitement:

- Provide resources that allow learners to practice their passions.

- Realize that young learners' passions may be fleeting and seek out ways to help them sustain passion.

- Communicate that if we tire of a passion, sometimes the learning in that moment is that we have tried something and discovered it is just not for us.

- Connect learners' passions to real-life contexts in which they can see in imagery and practice their passions come to life in the world.

- Build on passions as a place for young voice–led advocacy.

*

Social-emotional learning breeds social-emotional confidence. When learners recognize their social-emotional dispositions, they navigate learning with an understanding that belief in oneself means recognizing life's fragile moments, and they become better equipped to handle the discomfort of those fragile moments. Further, social-emotional confidence is universal. Humans emote for the same reasons and in the same situations, cultural context notwithstanding. Teachers can use social-emotional understanding as a common language to begin to treasure classroom culture.

Social-emotional learning breeds social-emotional confidence.

SIX

Treasure Culture

No culture can live if it attempts to be exclusive.

—MAHATMA GANDHI

*C*ulture is an umbrella term that encompasses the social behavior and norms found in human societies. It comprises the knowledge, beliefs, arts, laws, customs, capabilities, and habits of individuals in particular groups. For educators, culture takes on an even greater significance. We must start in our classrooms and build a culture that embraces *every* single being. We are made up of many cultures, and we should not exclude anyone. I am reminded of Mahatma Gandhi's belief that "no culture can live if it attempts to be exclusive." I have been fortunate to travel the world and experience many varied cultures. Personally, I find it exhilarating and thought-provoking to recognize how many traits, behaviors, and characteristics we share as humans, regardless of our cultural backgrounds. We all tend to act like other human beings in similar contexts. Why then is there such a struggle with culture in our classrooms?

It was during a visit with a group of early learners at another school that I first considered the cultures present in my own classroom and realized that valuing culture had to be intentional and teacher driven. We were outdoors, and the children were teaching me a modified version of hopscotch. As in every situation with young learners, I engaged them with questions. I wanted them to explain the game to me, show me how to play it, and invite me to join in. We quickly established rapport. While the game was going on, I noticed one quiet Little just looking at me. I watched as this same Little turned to a peer and whispered something, and they both giggled. Even as an adult, I felt a flush of confusion. One of the Littles, while giggling, said, "She's talking about your eyes. They are blue!" I replied, "They are blue. What color are your eyes?" He blinked rapidly, and I said, "I see them! They are the deepest root-beer brown eyes. So handsome!" He giggled again and said, "But why are yours blue?" I responded, "Well, my daddy and mommy both have blue eyes, so I also have blue eyes." During this conversation, a group of Littles had gathered and were staring and pointing at me and at one another. Finally, another Little said, "But we have the same hair. My eyes are not blue." The penny dropped. Yes, I have dark hair and light blue eyes. The group of Littles I was with all had beautiful black hair and varying shades of brown eyes and skin. Their teachers looked like them. I did not.

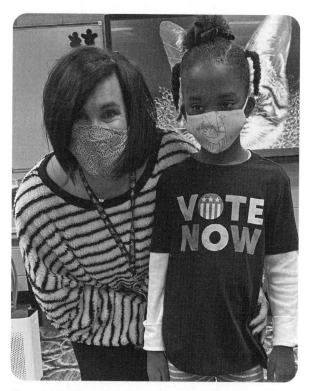

Our students come from different cultures, which we need to recognize and celebrate.

It was then that I knew I had to take a keen look at my classroom and my learners. I had to ensure that my resources, my classroom environment, and my behavior recognized and acknowledged every different culture within my classroom. I knew that I had to be intentional with my approach to these very same things so that my classroom's culture extended into the real-world relevance of culture. I had to address the challenges with culture and break them down so that as my Littles developed belief in themselves, they also developed a greater self-awareness born from acceptance. In short, I had to treasure the culture from the inside out.

NUDGE TO RELEVANCE

- How do you define *culture*?
- What challenges do you face with being culturally responsive in your teaching?

Culturally Responsive Teaching

The responsibility of fostering a belonging and believing learning space that is built on cultural inclusivity is on the teacher. While many teachers agree with the value of being culturally responsive in their teaching, it is often hard to imagine what culturally responsive teaching looks like in practice.

Culturally responsive teaching has found important relevance in education as a direct result of cultural shifts. However, being culturally responsive is not a new pedagogical idea. Ladson-Billings (1994) acknowledged Culturally Responsive Teaching as a pedagogy that recognizes the importance of including students' cultural references in all aspects of learning. There is not a specific formula for culturally responsive teaching, since every child is diverse and every family context is unique. However, to establish a culturally responsive foundation in our classroom, we need to address several matters.

There is not a specific formula for culturally responsive teaching, since every child is diverse and every family context is unique.

We must identify the values, principles, and beliefs in our classrooms and ensure they support diversity. We must also make sure that our methodologies reinforce these same principles in order that the culture created within our classroom translates to a greater appreciation of the ethos outside of our classroom. Creating a culturally responsive classroom stands on the back of the other tenets in this book. We must lean in and involve all our learners in building relationships and creating engaging opportunities for learning. We must value the implicit distinctions of our learners' behaviors without partiality. We must embrace the nuances of emotionality in each young learner to afford children a place of belonging.

Ginott (1972), a schoolteacher and psychologist, influenced my current teaching philosophy: "I have come to a frightening conclusion. I am the decisive element in the classroom. It is my personal approach that creates the climate. It is my daily mood that makes the weather. As a teacher, I possess tremendous power to make a child's life miserable or joyous. I can be a tool of torture or an instrument of inspiration. I can humiliate or humor, hurt or heal. In all situations it is my response that decides whether a crisis will be escalated or de-escalated, and a child humanized or de-humanized" (p. 15). This should be a charge for all teachers to treasure the culture of our classrooms and ensure that our classrooms embody a culturally relevant posture.

Acknowledge Your Predispositions

Teachers need to acknowledge that we carry with us implicit biases toward a host of different sociocultural ideas (De Houwer, 2019). By identifying and addressing the unconscious predispositions we carry, we can shift our focus to an appreciation of cultures, not solely an acceptance of them. To explore your personal implicit bias, I suggest spending some time among the curated information at the Project Implicit website (implicit.harvard.edu/implicit). Project Implicit is a nonprofit organization founded in 1988 that has since grown from three scientists to a cadre of researchers interested in social cognition. There are other resources you can explore, but I especially like the online test they administer to measure implicit bias. The results of my test have become much more than a topic of passing conversation with colleagues who have also taken the test. Instead, these results have prompted me to be intentional about ensuring I acknowledge, appreciate, and assimilate culture in my classroom. By reflecting on my own behavior, I am better positioned to be aware of cultural differences and how to navigate them in the classroom in an inclusive manner.

Expand Your Own Learning

While the world is vast, there are times when it can feel very, very close-knit. Teachers need to learn about cultures in an authentic way. Tap into community resources, such as small local theaters, historical venues, or local colleges and universities, for opportunities to be immersed in cross-cultural experiences. In your classroom, spend time leaning in, observing, and listening to your learners to see various patterns of communication and socialization that may need support and implicit understanding. For example, how do your young learners from diverse cultures:

- react to being called on to answer a question?
- use and respond to eye contact?
- interact on a social level?
- approach a challenging task?
- ask for help?
- exhibit emotion?
- react to attention?

Teachers have the ability to seek out opportunities to learn about cultures from a superficial perspective. However, to truly value culture, our view needs to be one of interest, understanding, and celebration. Read. Dig into the history of cultures. Travel. Visit places of worship, entertainment venues, and artistic and cultural institutions in your communities. Teachers have to do the groundwork to expand the learning, but it pays off in the heart work that will be embraced by the young learners in your classroom.

Curate Your Resources

The most immediate way to position yourself as a culturally responsive teacher is to take a close look at the resources in your classroom. Resources of the human variety, such as guest speakers, and the inanimate kind, such as literacy, need to reflect the values of the various cultures in your class. If you have never taken the time to look at your learners and compare their images to the images you share in your literacy choices, please do so now. You may find it eye-opening. After listening to Chimamanda Ngozi Adichie's TED Talk, "The Danger of a Single Story" (2009), I realized I had neglected a large population of my learners by not taking inventory of the images and story experiences I continually shared in my classroom. Although I grew up traveling the world and am married to someone from a different culture, I had faltered in punctuating learning for my diverse learners by not using mirrors of recognition in the books I chose. So, I changed that.

Late one afternoon, I sat and took an inventory of my books. I started with gender and then moved on to ethnicity. I had single titles that I used to anchor a holiday or a monthly celebration or a specific standard addressing culture. What I didn't have was an equitable, accessible library that recognized the diverse experiences, expectations, hopes, and history of the Littles who were in my classroom. Now I do. My library is a beautiful reminder of positive identity and possible future, no matter the skin color, gender, or ethnicity. Curating resources that are representative of different cultures—those present in your classroom and in the world— will give you tools to transform your teaching.

Transform Your Teaching

By learning about and reflecting on your own implicit biases, immersing yourself in relevant cultural experiences, and curating the resources you use to anchor lessons in your classroom, you will be well on your way to transforming teaching. Throughout this book, you will find whispers of opportunity to create relevance for all learners. I stress that these ideas are the intent to spur the content. Curriculum is the storehouse of the standards, lessons, assessments, and other academic content of classroom learning. When viewed through a culturally responsive lens, these parts may need to be challenged. While I am not suggesting that teachers throw out the curriculum, we do need to approach the curriculum from a place of cultural equity. Relying on our learners as experts is one way to challenge the status quo of curriculum. Finding ways to bridge the curriculum to advocacy and social action is another way we can transform our teaching to become more culturally responsive. While leaving the "must dos" intact, looking around the world provides a solid opportunity to transform teaching.

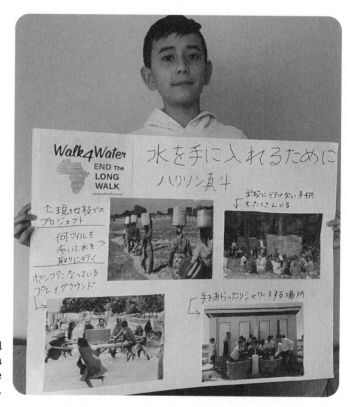

Promoting advocacy and social action is one way to transform our teaching to become more culturally responsive.

SEVEN

Look Around

It is looking at things for a long time that ripens you and gives you a deeper meaning.

—VINCENT VAN GOGH

V incent Van Gogh, a 19th-century Post-Impressionist painter, was known for his vivid colors. His artwork was a balanced blend of color, subject, and meaning. With his paintings, he focused on creating meaning rather than merely drawing a visual reaction. This is a fitting analogy for us teachers, as we must be bold in recognizing meaning around us. Instead of relying only on what our eyes tell us, we must look around for meaning to inspire relevant learning in our classrooms. For example, a rock that seems to be misplaced can create a context for your learners.

Looking Through a Teacher Lens

One evening, my family and I were getting ice cream in a small city outside our county. As I stepped out of the car, I looked down and saw a Minion looking up at me. Yes, one of those Minions! I picked it up, turned it over, and read "Cartersville Rocks" on the backside. I was curious. A simple Google search revealed a plethora of rock projects across communities. I would never have been aware of "joy rocks" had

I not been looking for meaning in my mysterious rock. I experienced more than a warm fuzzy feeling when I found this rock; I knew there had to be intent behind its placement. This and other rocks now have permanent relevance in my classroom. We have a rock-making station where my Littles can paint their joy rocks and write a little paragraph about what their rock means and where they are going to take it. The Littles then bring their rock someplace where someone else might find it and take it home. I imagine some of my Littles go back to their rock's spot to see if it's still there or if it has done its work of bringing joy to someone else.

Looking through a teacher lens—seeing things with teaching and learning in mind—can bring much curiosity and wonder in a classroom. When you begin to interact with the world at large through a teacher lens, the learning treasures you find will seem quite serendipitous. Often, you may not know what to do with them. Don't force the meaning. It is there. Keep the idea or object somewhere purposeful, and let the learning grow organically.

Consider setting up a "magic shelf" in your classroom. On the shelves of a bookcase I saved from being thrown out, I have a porcupine quill, a cow's shoulder blade, a bird's nest, freshly picked cotton, and a camel bell from Oman. These are all things I have found in my surroundings or received from others to use as inspiration in my classroom. (I certainly did not pluck a quill from a porcupine!) The magic shelf is a holding place that allows for relevance to be continual. Some of the items are purposeful, while others just sit there waiting for the moment to be introduced into the curriculum. When you start to observe and respond to your surroundings, your learners will, too.

Set up a "magic shelf" where you and your learners can display items of interest.

Even before the joy-rock experience, I have always been interested in rocks—stones, gems, minerals. I find a rock's journey amazing, and I like to look for stones on my travels. I add them to my magic shelf and label some of them with the name of the place where I found them. I have never mentioned to my Littles my rocks or why I have them or what they mean. One day, as I was thinking how badly I needed to dust my magic shelf, I discovered its true magic. My Littles had been adding to the shelf with artifacts from their own surroundings. They were being keen observers in their own settings—and adding a little bit of magic to our classroom. One Little had added a rock from a nearby lake; another had added a rock from the playground and duly labeled it with our school's name.

It's challenging to determine relevance for our learners, as what is significant to them shifts quickly. We need to recognize the continual shifts and be ready to frame, support, and encourage the relevant moments in our own lives to promote them in our learners' lives. Maybe artifacts aren't your thing. Maybe you need more of a push than a nudge to seek out the weird and wonderful in our world. To me, being relevant is being relational. We have to relate to our learners, even when they are little, in order to be relevant to them. I use two other areas in my room to foster relevance.

One such area is my Inspiration Station. It is ever evolving and ever growing. In my classroom it is simply a wall with fabric stapled to it and the words Inspiration Station. Nothing Pinterest-worthy. The real highlights are the scribbled ideas on napkins or scrap paper, the photos torn out of magazines, the drawings my Littles have made, the note cards, and so on. It is a place that inspires anyone who comes into the classroom. It inspires me! It is bold. It is full. It is layered. The scrawls and thoughts and relics all had meaning for someone in our classroom at one time or another, and by displaying them, they have the potential to be relevant to someone else, too.

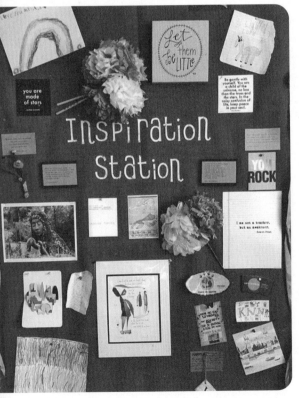

Another area in my classroom that gets a lot of attention is my Google Tree. How often have you experienced a lesson in which you asked a specific question directly related to a lesson, and a learner raised his or her hand only to share something that has nothing to do with the topic or the question you asked? Like when one of my Littles asked, "What happens to the dead animals you see on the road all the time? I mean, one day

Inspiration Station is where we display ideas, photos, or drawings that inspire us.

I see it and then the next morning it is gone." I thought, "What a great question. I have often wondered that myself."
It was not the right time to stop what was going on to figure out the answer, but it was then that the Google Tree sprouted. I had my Little write his question on a sticky note and post it by the computer. Since teachers are no longer the holders of knowledge, it is always likely that we will be asked a relevant question that we simply cannot answer.

My Google Tree is a receptacle for my Littles' wonderings, burning questions, or passion ideas. Each year the tree looks different. Sometimes it is a paper tree growing up the wall on a corner in my classroom; other times it's a branch in a pot. The leaves or snowflakes or birds (you get the picture) that sit on the branches of the tree are the questions my Littles have. Through each season of learning, their questions gain depth and become more relevant to our content.

Learners post their "I wonder" questions on the branches of our Google Tree and research the answers whenever time allows.

This means they are connecting what is relevant to them with the current learning. I'm not responsible for answering their questions. The Google Tree is their first go-to place when they have free time or come in early in the morning. Sometimes they want to share their learning with the class during morning meeting, and sometimes they don't. I often browse the tree to look for meaning and think about how I can integrate their small but relevant wonders into a larger experience for them. Sometimes, the tree goes through a season without answers, and that's okay. The point of the tree is to value my Littles' ideas and questions and thus value what is relevant to them.

NUDGE TO RELEVANCE
- What do you notice in your own environment that could bring relevance to your teaching?
- What can you establish in your classroom that gives your learners ownership of the things that are relevant to them?

In Pursuit of Wonder

If we open our eyes and look around, there really is wonder all around. It is our responsibility as teachers to remove the walls of our classrooms and invite the wonder of the world inside. Much of what becomes relevant in our classrooms depends on the lens teachers use. If you are curious, you inspire curiosity in your young learners as well. If you are questioning, you allow space for young learners to question. If you see connections in big ideas, your Littles will start to connect their learning. For some teachers, these practices are innate. They were instilled by a teacher or by a circumstance. For others, they need to be intentional. Following are some small ways you can start to bring the outside world into your classroom and provoke wonder in your learners.

Daily Wonder Share a photograph—or, even better, an artifact—of something a little offbeat or unsuspected. Provide time for Littles to sketch the object and respond to a reflection prompt, such as:

- *What do you think it is?*
- *Who might have used it?*
- *What do you think it is made of?*
- *How could you use it?*
- *What could it be named?*
- *Where did it come from?*

A simple wonder, such as these, is a prompt for thinking, writing, and exploring the world. Some of the items that are "Hall of Fame" wonders in my classroom include a Zulu warrior flyswatter, an antique metal detector, a praying mantis egg case, and baking potato spears. A brief moment of looking around transfers into rich conversation. It calls for the use of historical resources. It promotes understanding of cultures. Most important for me, it fosters a strong sense of curiosity in my learners.

What Do You Spot? Have you ever looked at the keypad in an elevator and noticed that the number 13 is missing? I have. "What do you spot?" is a hook task that can propel learners far in their thinking. I use images and experiences from every nook and cranny of the world and present them to my learners and simply ask: *What do you spot?* It can be translated into an "I see, I think, I wonder" strategy, but sometimes just letting the wonder linger is all you need to spark curiosity. In my phone's photo album, I have image after image of things that make wonderful "what do you spot" opportunities. The intent is set by you. The wonder is set by your learners.

Language of Wonder If teachers use the language of wonder, it takes a pervasive stance in the classroom. "I wonder how old this text is." "I wonder why the lights go off when we don't move for a long time." "I wonder why Amelia Earhart felt that way." I do not oppose teachers doing some of the talking in the classroom, especially if our talking inspires a sense of wonder in our young learners. These conversations and shared thoughts are the building blocks of who young learners are becoming.

Bring the World In I visited Disneyland some years ago. As I was walking along the shopping area, I happened upon a Lego display of Beauty and the Beast. It was life-size and flawless. Of course, I took a photograph. Upon returning to school, I told my Littles about my trip. (It was to a professional learning conference, and my Littles are always intrigued when I tell them I am learning, too.) I shared the photograph and asked, "How many Legos do you think it took to build this?" After the predictable refrains of "one million" died down, I charged them with this task:

This photograph of Beauty and the Beast made from Legos sparked many relevant, learning-rich activities in my classroom.

1. How can we figure out how many Legos were used?
2. Do that.

This "struggle task" (one that requires heavy thinking, consistent effort, and determination) lasted for several weeks. I didn't expect my Littles to actually come up with the correct answer. In fact, I have no idea how many Lego bricks were used. But the prompt elicited some amazing thinking that introduced concepts of area, perimeter, and even volume. These are quite lofty mathematical thoughts for young learners. Littles love building blocks, and my sharing with them something from the outside world that was relevant to their interests resulted in rich learning opportunities. One Little researched 25 of the most amazing Lego statues around the world. Another built smaller statues and brought them in for peers to calculate the number of bricks used.

A simple look around became the basis for a relevant problem-solving experience. Daily, we have opportunities to bring the world into our classrooms. We simply must look up, look down, and look around.

EIGHT

Explore Experiences

You can be the architect of moments that matter.

—CHIP HEATH

An unexpected snowfall justified interrupting our lesson to allow children to experience this rare and joyful occasion.

Some of the most authentic learning experiences come from unexpected, spontaneous, or unpredictable moments that take us off script. The moments that leave us joyful, knowing that what just occurred was more important than the planned lesson, yet connect to the learning at hand. Experiences can be as simple as noticing a gaggle of geese on the school grounds and joining your Littles on a supervised "wild goose chase" during a literacy lesson or heading outside for the season's first snowfall (which is so rare in our Southern state, it must be experienced). Or they can be much more expansive, such as student-driven service learning, authentic competitions, or community-based experiences.

We must be willing to embrace these experiences and seek out ways to integrate them into our curriculum. Too often we dismiss these serendipitous moments instead of capitalizing on them. There is power in moments that provoke emotion, connection, and memories.

One time we were on a class outing, celebrating a capstone event in which we had partnered with a local theater to create an interactive preshow learning experience for even littler learners in the community. As we traveled by school bus, a mere 26 miles from school, I listened as the children squealed, "Look at these tall buildings!" "Do you think this is Paris?" "Why do you think cities have tall buildings?" "How much do you think the electricity is?" "What happens if our bus breaks down?" Their excitement made me cherish the experience, because as a teacher, I don't relish riding on a school bus at all. When we arrived at the theater, there was a single-entry door adjacent to a revolving door. The person who welcomed us instructed that "children must use the single-entry door." I found that rather peculiar, but obliged. We spent the morning engaging younger learners, observing, and participating in a live theater production and debriefed with sack lunches behind the stage. When we were finally ready to depart the building, the revolving door caught Mariah's eye. This seven-year-old Little turned to me and asked, "What is that?" I replied, "It's a revolving door. Have you never seen one?" She responded, "Never!" with an eagerness that I knew I had to satisfy. With that, Mariah

Meaningful experiences can come from something as simple as taking a walk on the school grounds.

and I entered the moving door. We went around three or four times while everyone else boarded the bus. As I stepped out, I turned to see Mariah's face emanating pure joy and suddenly realized she didn't know how to get out on her own. I laughingly shouted, "Mariah, you have to jump out on the next pass—ready?" And as she came around again, she leapt out, almost bowling me over. Being dramatic, Mariah pretended to catch her breath—although I am sure the experience really was breathtaking for her. It was such a small thing, to allow that exploration. It wasn't contrived. Authentic experiences, no matter how small, create relevant connections with our learners. This Little experienced something that brought her wonder.

We have the opportunity to invent experiences with much of what we do in classrooms. If we plant seeds of exploration and seek out opportunities for our learners and embrace the experiences with authenticity, our classrooms transcend the four walls and our Littles begin to appreciate who they can become.

Cultivating Authentic Experiences

Sometimes I listen to my Littles and feel a twinge of despair when they speak about their experiences. Today's generation of learners is immersed in digital worlds of contrived contexts. I often feel they are missing out on the amazing world around us and the people and things that make it so remarkable. Authentic experiences are more content-driven, but they start with a willingness on our part to search for that little nugget that will connect to our teaching and engage our learners.

Cultivating authentic, relevant experiences for learners can be arduous. It is messy and time-consuming. It requires so much effort. Yet, when we sow seeds that lead to unforgettable experiences for our learners, the painstaking process of creating them is worth it. Even the smallest occurrences can connect the real world to the learning in our classrooms. We must be willing to scour resources to find content that coincides with our current learning. We must be perceptive about relevant matters. Following are some ideas for cultivating experiences.

Currently Speaking

Some teachers seem to have difficulty seeing the relevance of world news in their elementary classrooms. They neatly tuck away current local, state, and world events on the shelf next to show-and-tell, instead of embracing and utilizing the news as an intentional talking, teaching, and learning point. Young learners love current events. If you don't think so, lean in and listen to their conversations. Littles love to talk about stuff that is relevant to the local community ("Hey, did you have a tornado warning at your house?" "Well, I know tornadoes need warm weather, and it was warm outside.") or in the greater world ("I saw this animal from Australia that looks like he is smiling! It's called a quokka.") If your learners are not having these conversations, build a space for them to engage in discourse. Do your own investigating and create a "Currently Speaking Corner" where children can explore and discuss trends and hot topics. Search news sites and not just the headlines. Click on the lifestyle, entertainment, and sports tabs. Review what is trending on Twitter. Check out the Amazon Best Sellers lists. While these prompts may not connect to your current classroom learning, they are an opportunity to spark an authentic experience, such as in the following examples.

Littles love to talk about stuff that is relevant to the local community or in the greater world.

The Retirement of Dandelion as a Color

After reading the picture book *The Day the Crayons Quit,* by Drew Daywalt, my learners came upon a news article about Crayola retiring one of its crayon colors, dandelion, and replacing it with a shade of blue. My learners eagerly took on the persona of the dandelion crayon and crafted their own letters to the company, either pleading to remain in the box or expressing why they were happy to leave the box. To further this lesson, my Littles used their creative thinking and submitted their suggestions for the new color.

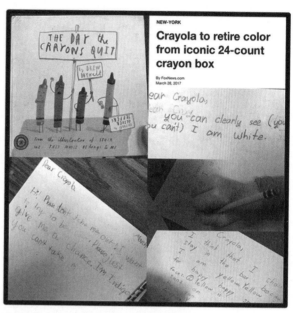

My Littles wrote letters to Crayola in response to the company's decision to retire one of its colors.

Gaspard the Fox

While mining for ideas, I stumbled upon a BBC News article about a man, Zeb Soanes, who befriended an injured fox that appeared at his flat in North London. I knew this was something that would engage my learners. First, I had my Littles investigate the character traits of foxes in storybooks. We then looked at character traits of real-life foxes and compared them with the fictional foxes' traits. I posed this question: *Do foxes get a bad rap in storybooks?* I then introduced my learners to Gaspard the Fox, the name that Soanes gave the fox who repeatedly returned to his flat. At some point, I reached out to Soanes and told him that we were using his story in my classroom. He shared the etymology of Gaspard's name—which is French—and I, in turn, shared it with my Littles. We dabbled in beginning French and eventually wrote letters to Gaspard with questions we had brainstormed based on our learning about foxes. (I hope as you read this, you recognize that experiences, while intentional, are often student-led, chaos-driven, and magical in their authenticity.) With the help of his human friend, Gaspard wrote letters back to each of my Littles. My Littles became amateur zoologists. They researched fox behavior and analyzed pros and cons of urban foxes and domesticated foxes. Ultimately, my Littles debated the original prompt: *Do foxes get a bad rap in storybooks?* They then created public service announcement presentations defending their position based on their total experience, starting with their introduction to Gaspard and ending with guided research. On a side note, many of my learners began asking their grown-ups for a pet fox (yikes!), and several came across fox-rescue organizations. This learning journey is a testament to the power of bringing real-world, authentic experiences to the classroom.

Daily School News Program

If your school has a news program, newsletter, podcast, or other media-driven expression of school events, this could be a perfect way to give young learners a distinct purpose and audience and to make learning more relevant. Several years ago, my Littles took on the daily production of a live news broadcast that was simulcast in all the classrooms. When my class was charged with this responsibility, I immediately knew it was a special opportunity to invest in everything I believe is relevant for young learners. My Littles created the framework for the broadcast, wrote and edited the script, performed as anchors, directed the show, operated the camera, managed the split screen and the green screen technology to manipulate the background that viewers see, and so on. They were seven-year-olds and were able to do all this after a week of training and with very little continued oversight by me. They incorporated daily fun holidays, weather reports, thoughtful Thursday reflections, student spotlights, and breaking news. It was a major undertaking, and it all unfolded within the first 30 minutes of school before the tardy bell rang. It was probably one of the best daily experiences my learners ever had, and it absolutely encouraged a sense of responsibility, reliability, independence, interdependence, resilience, and joyfulness.

Putting on a daily news program made learning relevant and meaningful to these young learners.

Community-Connected Experiences

Communities celebrate schools and lift them up in learning. Seek out opportunities within your local community or surrounding areas. Several years ago, I connected with the Kathy and Ben Bernhardt Theatre for the Very Young in Atlanta, Georgia. The relationship between the theater and my classroom (through the Alliance Theatre Dramaturgy by Students program) is rich in literature, collaboration, and educational outreach. One year, the literature selection for the theater performance was *Beautiful Blackbird*, by Ashley Bryan. Another year, it was an original production called *La Tortuga and the Hare*, and yet another year it was a commissioned piece titled *In My Granny's Garden*.

Each year, my Littles have the opportunity to work with an actor from the theater and learn strategies for engaging the audience, preview scripts, and connect the production to specific learning standards in the classroom. Using each piece of literature as an anchor, learners

In collaboration with a local theater company, my Littles designed interactive "creation stations" to engage very young theatergoers.

explore its cultural elements—music, art, science, and social studies—and use them to design learner-driven "creation stations." My learners then present these interactive stations during a collaborative preshow event for community children, from infancy to age 5. For example, for *In My Granny's Garden*, one group of Littles created a sensory vegetable garden using a variety of materials to teach texture and color. Another group made an interactive book that taught preschool children about colors and vocabulary words for common vegetables. Still another group performed a simple rhythmic dance using props to simulate a seed growing into a plant. After the shared preshow presentation, we all watched the production together as part of the audience. The actual experience was so much more involved than words can express.

Other experiences that connect our learners and communities include service learning projects and service outreach opportunities. Many organizations welcome young volunteers who are eager to learn about stepping outside themselves. Children can help make lunches for a summer food program, create cards for elder facilities, or participate in something that goes beyond volunteer outreach to true service learning, in which young learners recognize and support a solution to a real-world problem in their community or in the greater world. Young learners can get the most out of these relevant moments. Plant the seed of exploration in children and encourage them to forge their own paths as they seek out social issues and needs that they care about in their communities.

Competitions

I love to introduce competition into the classroom. A competition with an authentic purpose and woven into learning brings optimal engagement. As with other experiences, competitions take a level of commitment from the teacher. Teachers and learners alike need to appreciate the process and embrace the messy ambiguity that competitions often demand. The intent behind participating in competitions is not to win, but rather to have an authentic audience. Of course, winning is a wonderful bonus if it happens, as it did for my second graders.

My Littles participated in the Evergreen Packaging Made by Milk competition. The theme of the competition was inventions, and the task was to create an object out of repurposed milk cartons. The learning focus was on sustainability. A group of young learners decided to create a model of *The General*, a Civil War steam locomotive. Over a six-week stretch of brainstorming, problem-solving, and collaborating, they did indeed manufacture a replica of this steam engine using 1,120 recycled milk cartons from the school cafeteria. My learners won a national prize, which they chose to use toward an ice cream party. But what they really received was hard-earned knowledge, as evidenced by their comments:

- "I learned that you always need to be willing to change the design even when you think you're doing what you want. It might be better with changes or what you're doing doesn't really work so you need to change it." (Tyler, age 7)
- "Sometimes when you work with people, you need to listen and not just talk because they might have good ideas." (Cullen, age 7)

Using milk cartons collected from the cafeteria, students built a replica of *The General*, a Civil War steam locomotive, for a competition.

- "I learned we have to stop and check our work because we had too many cartons on one side and we didn't know until we had glued it all. We had to start over, but we should have looked first and then it would have been okay." (Malcolm, age 7)

As their teacher, I learned I had to let them fail to succeed.

There are many competitions open to learners, including:

- **Doodle for Google** – An annual creative competition in which learners create their own Google Doodle (www.google.com/doodles)

- **K–12 Inventure Prize** – An annual event that encourages learners to identify real-world problems and design innovative solutions to these problems (www.k12inventure.org)

While finding competitions for young learners is a bit challenging (grown-ups haven't all figured out how much Littles can do yet!), keep in mind that many local community agencies host competitions. Through networking, teachers can also organize their own competitions among classrooms or schools. The possibilities are endless.

Walk for Africa

Experiences do not need to be limited. Remember: Young learners may be little, but they are fierce. In fact, they are at the optimal age to begin connecting experience to social action and advocacy. As we nurture and encourage student voice, I want to share with you one experience that illustrates the power of each of these ideas working together to reach and teach young learners.

Literature can be an intentional and powerful resource to launch an experience for young learners. During an integrated learning collaboration, I selected a novel, *A Long Walk to Water*, to connect the many ideas my 4th-grade class was exploring. At a pivotal part in this particular story, I could sense my Littles begin to comprehend the completely barren area the characters were living in and how access to water was impossible. This was a tough concept for children who always have water bottles at their disposal; but something was starting to spark. I invited a guest speaker from a nonprofit organization that brings potable water to parched areas of Africa. My Littles' interest grew.

At one point during our reading, a Little asked, "What can we do to help?" I responded, "What do you think we can do?" The class immediately offered ideas, such as send water to Africa or build a machine to dig for water. I asked them to think more deeply about ways we could help. The next day, when we went back to brainstorming ideas, the conversation was rich but the ideas lacked finesse. One Little suggested we open a lemonade stand and raise money to send to Africa. After researching the cost of digging a well, she conceded, "That's a lot of lemonade." I encouraged them to keep thinking. Even as their teacher, I didn't have a solution. Then I heard a Little say, "Well, you know, I did a race once with my dad, and I think the money went to someone who needed shelter or something." The spark caught.

Over the next several weeks, my Littles planned a walk for Africa. (Looking back, they were cutting edge since this walk was virtual when virtual races were not the norm!) My Littles spent time researching and piecing together a plan. They designed T-shirts. They advertised the walk. They learned about the power of social media and created a hashtag to connect walkers who would participate. They recorded registrations. They created a learning brochure about water for participants. They handwrote thank-you letters to each and every walker, and sent them along with the brochure and T-shirt. They decided to donate the money to the nonprofit organization that had visited us earlier in the month. I provided teacher facilitation and

Inspired by the book *A Long Walk to Water*, my Littles organized a walk to raise money to build a well in a village in Burkina Faso.

oversight, but it was from a stance of assistance, not direction. What ensued was an inaugural classroom service learning project, Walk for Africa, which raised $2,200—enough to have a well dug in Burkina Faso. Remember, this all started with a book and a question, "What can we do to help?" Much later, we received confirmation of our efforts in a postcard that included the coordinates to the well we had funded. My Littles also received recognition from the county Board of Commissioners.

Sometimes small sparks grow into wildfires. When we encourage young learners to use their voice, they too can move toward social action. These experiences are the most memorable ones. While this experience started with a novel and a question, I affirm that if we allow our learners the freedom to explore and are willing to embrace the journey with them, their experiences become a mirror held up in front of our learners, showing them exactly who they can become.

Authentic experiences should be relevant and, in my opinion, not replicated. After experiences my Littles engage in ripple through the school, I am often asked, "Are you going to do that again?" As much as I would love to lead more learners through the experiences former students have participated in, I typically do not. Experiences are born from a place of bold relevance and context, and I am not sure if regurgitating them would have the same impact. I prefer to plant seeds of possibility with my learners and wait for them to initiate the experiences.

I prefer to plant seeds of possibility with my learners and wait for them to initiate the experiences.

For many experiences, there are no formal lesson plans. The lesson plan is lean in, understand, take care of their emotions, ensure a place of cultural sensitivity, and look around. Thus, while exact adventures are challenging to duplicate, I am confident that my Littles will always find new paths to explore. It is important to interject here that I recognize that my learners are young. I am aware of the parameters of their social-emotional capacities and their cognitive abilities. I also recognize that when we forge authentic experiences for our learners, there is sometimes a hesitation regarding content, and teachers often fret about topics that are sensitive or mature or just plain difficult. However, I believe that if our Littles speak it, it is important to them, and we as teachers have an obligation to address these sticky contexts with fairness, truth, and the space for learners to do the thinking, the questioning, and the creating.

NINE

Putting It All Together

Unleash the Wheesht!

*W*heesht is an homage to my family's Scottish heritage. It is a word that tells someone to be quiet. In your classrooms, it may sound like "Shhh!" or "Not now" or "We can't speak about that at school" or "Hold on to your thoughts. I'm talking." One of the easiest ways to capitalize on relevant moments is to let your learners talk, or "unleash the wheesht!" I allow my Littles to engage in conversation as they work, even if it doesn't connect to the task at hand. The sidebar comments or the rush of conversation as they are starting their day or transitioning to something new all have merit in our classroom.

There is something to be said about allowing social discourse among learners—especially those conversations during which we teachers do not utter a word, we just listen. It's so easy to hush our learners. But when our Littles are bursting with questions, keep in mind that their questions give us great insight into what matters to them. If we teach them to let things flow—and if we actually let things flow in the classroom—Littles will learn how to ask purposeful questions, how to discern what is fair and adequate to speak about, how to defend themselves, and how to engage in debate. This is especially true if we don't exert our adult opinions on the topic at hand. Most of the time, Littles actually model how adults should share differing opinions or ideas. Similarly, by not "wheeshting" our learners, we promote the value of student voice in the classroom.

Sometimes the topics that Littles want to discuss bear witness to a more mature perspective. Take, for example, a recent exchange my Littles had during our Daily Wonder exploration one morning. I heard one Little utter, "I don't like when people say I am Black." My ears perked up, and I wondered where this conversation was going. Instead of hushing his voice, I picked up my phone to record the conversation. (I often do this so I can later reflect on these random moments of learning.)

He continued, "See this crayon? It says *black*. I am not black."

Another Little said, "You're brown!"

To which another classmate chimed in, "Well, I'm brown too, but look"—she put her arm up next to her friend's—"we aren't even the same brown."

One Little who was listening started to look through her crayon box and said, "Well, you know what? I am White, but I am not white like this." She held up a white crayon.

By now, the conversation had attracted the interest of more than half of my classroom. One of my little boys asked, "I wonder why we are all different colors?"

Laughingly, one of the original speakers said, "Well, dogs are all different colors, but they are all dogs."

Then the conversation grew a little less innocent as one Little observed, "But sometimes people with different color skin are treated differently, and that's not fair."

"You're right, it's not fair. How come only people are treated differently?"

I held my breath.

"Yeah, because we are all different. Even White people and Brown people and Black people and peach people."

"Peach people?"

"Yes, look. I am peach. I am not white."

"But we don't say 'peach people.'"

"But we are all different white and different black and different peach and different brown."

A wave of emotion rose inside me as I recognized the promise of the world chatting in my classroom. Then, the question came:

> "Why do you think we are all different colors? How come some of us are lighter and darker and have freckles?"

> "And some of us have black hair and yellow hair."

> "I think a long time ago some people lived in the sun. Like when we are in the sun, our skin turns darker. But I don't know why that would mean different people get mad when we are not the same."

Then the conversation started to taper off.

> "Well, at least there are crayons with all of our colors. Look, this is me, and this is you, and this is you . . ."

> Then one Little, who was sitting across the room from this discussion, shared, "Well, I think I am more white because I ate a lot of salt when I was little."

What I witnessed was like a microcosm of adults having a conversation. There's always that one oblivious person who doesn't really pay attention, while others are more intent on the discussion at hand. And you know what? It was discussion. It flowed. No one had their feelings hurt—and sure, there was a bit of a perspective challenge going on—but it allowed learners to think, to process, and to have some social discourse without an adult influencing their ideas or shushing their voices.

When we teachers stop the flow of conversation and do not simply listen, we inadvertently promote the notion that our Littles' voices don't matter, and we lose out on unexpected, tangential learning. We lose out on relevance. Communication is one of the 21st-century learning skills, and it's a challenge to teach the concept of communication with contrived experiences or simulations. It is much more beneficial to witness these skills develop authentically. In fact, had this conversation gone any differently, it would have been a prime instance in which I could have interjected a teachable moment about listening, respecting others' opinions, perspective, fact-checking—or a plethora of other important discourse skills.

Building an expectation of social discourse means creating a relevant awareness in your learners. Littles likely won't bring in breaking-news stories (although sometimes they do!). However, as I've mentioned, tapping into sources of current events can set the stage for your Littles to have a reason to engage in social conversation with a prescribed intent. Ultimately, the most profitable conversations are the organic ones that stem from a Little's own voice. It is all too common, though, that learners are compliant and hesitant to talk outside of learning boundaries. Teachers need to provide a little direction to arrive at the point where social discourse is a daily practice.

The most profitable conversations are the organic ones that stem from a Little's own voice.

It would be unfair to suggest that all social conversations go exactly as the one I have shared. When Littles engage in free discussion, you'll have many relevant, social-emotional teachable moments. I find Littles can be as emotionally charged as some adults when they share stories or experiences. We must understand that through social conversations, we have the ability to witness and shape socially relevant responses, too. There are instances when we, as teachers, must interject and guide the conversation and use the discussion as a teachable moment. If someone says something that is a personal attack or is heading down a path that will likely cause terribly hurt feelings, anger, or worse, then I absolutely will interject and redirect. Yet, when learning is significant to Littles, they discover a comfortable belonging, a strong belief in their abilities, and an overwhelming sense of who they can become through the vessel of relevance.

So as we put everything together—from leaning in, improving understanding, tackling emotionality, treasuring culture, looking around, and exploring experiences—our classrooms evolve into contexts in which young learners bear witness to the importance of being relevant with them. This relevance is not artificial and is not limited to within the classroom walls. Relevant matters reveal the opinions and behaviors of young learners and illustrate who they are becoming right before our eyes.

TEN

Relevant Lessons

As teachers, we must find what is relevant with our learners. Intricacies in the curriculum and goals within the standards still leave room for weaving in significant lessons that highlight the relevant matters in our classrooms. The lessons that follow are merely examples of what you can develop for your learners. The lesson topics are not meant to be singular, isolated tasks in your classrooms. Rather, they are meant to be starting points for building the framework of belonging, believing, and becoming. Try these lessons with your learners. Feel free to adapt any part of them, whether the mentor literature, the engage task, or the questioning. Make them your own. Embrace the ambiguity of not knowing how the conversations and the learning may evolve. Just make them relevant.

Intricacies in the curriculum and goals within the standards still leave room for weaving in significant lessons that highlight the relevant matters in our classrooms.

Weave relevant matters into your lessons to engage young learners.

Superpower Words

Overview

Empower learners to use their voices to affirm their place in the classroom. Exploring positive and negative words with young learners allows them to see the influence word choice has on their voice.

Relevance

This lesson establishes the power of words. It creates a framework for learners to reflect on the message that words send. Understanding the power of words and how we use them gives credence to intentional learning and social dialogue in the classroom.

Learning Tools

- *Words and Your Heart,* by Kate Jane Neal
- square paper coasters, cardstock, or other medium for learners to design*
- pencils and color markers
- blank, white labels
- hole puncher and string (optional)

* If you intend to display learners' creations, punch two holes at the top of each square. On some of the squares, put random marks on their surface before sharing with learners.

Engage

Ask learners:

- *What are some words you hear when you do something well?*
- *How do those words make you feel?*
- *What are some words you hear when you make a mistake?*
- *How do those words make you feel?*

Build Knowledge

Read aloud *Words and Your Heart*. After reading, ask learners:

- *What words do we use with our friends? Our family? Our teachers?*
- *How can words help a situation?*
- *How can words hurt a situation?*
- *What kinds of words should we use when?*

Apply

Tell learners: *Words can be a commitment. We are going to commit to a word that is going to be your superpower word. This word is going to help you in situations in which things seem to go wrong.*

Guide learners through the following steps. You may model these steps, but for authentic creations, it is best to coach little learners through any struggles they may experience.

1 Tell learners: *There is one rule for you to follow with this task. You will be using a pencil to begin, and you may not erase any of the marks that you create. This is to remind you that we all have marks. We have things that we are proud of, and we make mistakes. We are human beings, and no one is perfect.*

2 Give each learner a square piece of paper. Say: *Each of you has a piece of paper. If you look around, you will notice that some of your papers already have marks on them. Those marks are there to make you think of the words that we use. When we use words with others, we cannot take them back. We need to always remember to use positive, superpower words.*

3 Have learners draw four lines that connect the sides of their paper. Say: *This is to remind you that words connect ideas and people. Be creative with your lines. They can be zigzag or curved. Your words are your words and are designed by you.*

4 Next, have learners draw two circles that overlap the lines in some way. Tell them: *These circles are to remind you that relationships are important. We create positive, strong relationships when we use superpower words and turn those words into actions.*

5 Next, prompt learners to draw an organic shape. Explain that an organic shape is not like a square or a triangle or a circle. Say: *This shape is to remind you that sometimes the words we use are unexpected. We all get angry or upset or frustrated. Sometimes we even blurt out a word because we are so excited.*

6 Tell learners: *Using our words together is powerful. Find two friends that you can connect your square with. Connect your square to your friends' squares by drawing a new line or shape to connect them. You can continue with a line that someone has already started.* (You will likely need to model this.)

7 Explain: *Sometimes we use our words in a poor manner. It surprises our friends. Sometimes friends do the same to us. It can make us a little uncomfortable. To remind you what it feels like when someone uses a word to hurt your feelings, trade your square with someone else. It is going to make you feel funny, but that's okay. I want you to be uncomfortable.*

Use string to connect and display learners' superpower words.

8 Now that each child has a new square, tell learners they are going to add color to it. Say: *Sometimes our words are misunderstood even if we use the correct words. This step is to remind you that being messy is okay. The process of understanding one another can be messy, but it can also end up being wonderful.* Note: As learners complete their squares, have them place the squares at an assigned spot in the classroom.

9 Tell learners: *We have all created colorful squares. We learned how words create marks on our hearts. We learned how words connect us to others. We learned how words help us work together. We learned how words can be unexpected sometimes. We learned that sometimes our words are messy. Now it's time to give our own superpower word a place of commitment. Remember, I shared at the beginning of this lesson that we are going to commit to a superpower word. I want you to think of your personal superpower word. Remember all of the things we learned about words and the power they have.*

10 Invite learners to find a square that appeals to them, a square that they like. Maybe they like the color, maybe they like the pattern, or maybe they aren't sure why they like it. Tell learners that's okay. Say: *Look at the square you've chosen. Is there a word that belongs on that square? I am going to give each of you a blank label. I want you to think about all we have learned about words and their power today. You are going to pick your superpower word and write it on this label. This is your commitment.*

Reflect

Invite learners to share their superpower words with the class. Make these words part of a larger display by linking them together with a string through the holes punched at the top. Use these words as a reference when encouraging learners to share ideas or navigate social discord in the classroom.

Push Through

Overview

As learners strive to believe in themselves, it is important to explore ideas and opportunities that develop a growth mindset and teach perseverance, even when things are challenging.

Relevance

This lesson introduces mantras and allows learners to reflect on routines they can develop when things get challenging for them as they establish belief in their abilities.

Learning Tools

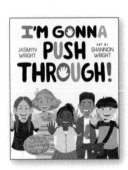

- a photo of a hedgehog
- *I'm Gonna Push Through!,* by Jasmyn Wright
- "Our 2017 'Push Through' GAP Kids Back to School" commercial on YouTube (https://www.youtube.com/watch?v=A2SolFMl94E)
- paper and pencils
- art supplies for learners' visual art creation (e.g., paper, markers, paint)

Engage

Share an image of a hedgehog. Invite learners to describe how holding a hedgehog might feel. (Possible responses include *pokey, prickly, hard, ouch.*) Have them think of a time when they felt like something in their life was prickly or pokey or hard or ouch. (Possible responses include personal examples of challenging situations, both big and small.)

Ask learners: *What did you do during those times?*

Explain that to protect itself, a hedgehog might try to flee. It can also roll itself up into a ball as a defense. Tell learners: *Things often get prickly in our lives, whether we are learning something new or find something that bugs us or are just having a bad day that doesn't seem to be going our way. Unlike hedgehogs, we can't roll up into a ball, and running away from our challenges doesn't make us any stronger. There are things we can do to push through these times.*

Build Knowledge

Read aloud *I'm Gonna Push Through!* Encourage learners to call back, "I'm gonna push through" during the parts of the story that support this. After reading, ask learners:

- *Do you recognize any of these people? Isn't it amazing to think that even though they become well-known, they, too, had challenges in life?*

- *What do you notice about every situation in our book when things were prickly?*

Tell learners: *"I'm gonna push through" is a mantra. A mantra is a word or a statement that is repeated over and over. In this book, we learn that a mantra can help us push through challenges.*

Apply

Encourage each learner to create a mantra that he or she can use when things get challenging.

1 Show learners the "Our 2017 'Push Through' GAP Kids Back to School" commercial on YouTube. It features the call-back cheer that was the seed for the book.

2 Ask learners: *What are some situations that are prickly or challenging and that we need to push through? What are some things we can do when things get challenging?* (Often learners will share the "correct" answers. Lean in and share examples of getting upset, quitting, crying,

Children's designed mantras

and so on, so learners realize that when things get challenging, we don't always push through or find an appropriate way to address the challenge.)

3 Provide time for learners to brainstorm mantras they can use when things get challenging.

4 Distribute art supplies and invite learners to create a visual art representation of their mantra.

Put learners' mantras on display so children can refer to them as needed.

Reflect

Invite learners to share their mantras with the class. Afterward, display the mantras in the classroom where learners can easily refer to them throughout the school year. During morning meetings, engage in a class mantra shout-out. Share an observation you made in which a learner was challenged and used a mantra to push through.

From the Inside Out

Overview

Learners need to have a safe space to feel a sense of belonging. Often, the character traits young learners share on the outside do not tell the whole story about them.

Relevance

This reflective lesson provides a place for learners to think about their strengths and their weaknesses as they pertain to social-emotional thinking.

Learning Tools

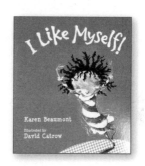

- hand mirror
- *I Like Myself!,* by Karen Beaumont
- small paper bags
- pencils, markers, crayons
- index cards, cut in half

Engage

Give learners a hand mirror to pass around the classroom. As they do so, ask them to think about the prompts below. Don't allow for responses, just reflective thought time.

- *What do you see?*
- *What do you like about what you see?*
- *Are there things about yourself that you do not see?*
- *When people see you, what do they see?*
- *What things do you wish people would see about you?*

Build Knowledge

Read aloud *I Like Myself!* After reading, ask learners:

- *Think back to looking in the mirror. What do you like about yourself?* (Allow learners to share both physical and nonphysical traits.)
- *Are there ever things about ourselves that people do not see?* (Of course there are.)
- *Give some examples of things people do not see. For example, people don't see that I worry a lot. What about you?*

Apply

1 Provide each learner with a small paper bag. Invite children to decorate the outside of the bag with three to five words, phrases, or pictures that describe how they think other people see them. Tell learners: *Think about how your teacher sees you, how your grown-ups see you, how your friends see you, how your coaches see you.*

2 Next, hand out three half index cards to each learner. Say: *Think about the things that people don't see about you that you wish they would. For example, people don't see that I am a worrywart. I wish they knew this about me.* Have learners write one thing they wish people knew about them on each card.

3 Have learners place the cards in their paper bag. Tell them that the outside of the bag is to remind us of the things we can see in one another. The inside of the bag is to remind us of the things we wish people saw in us.

4 Prompt: *Why do you think it is important to let the things inside the bag become a part of what people see in us?*

**Words outside the paper bag describe
how other people see us.**

Reflect

Solicit responses to the prompt from learners who are willing to share. This is a very private, personal task for some learners. Some may not want to share their thoughts. Display the bags in a place where learners can access them. Provide extra index cards for learners to use when they observe a trait or behavior in a peer that they want to celebrate by placing it in that child's bag. Periodically, allow learners to look inside their bags for traits others may have added and to reflect on their personal growth as it relates to the characteristics they identified.

I Am . . . Like a . . .

Overview

Learners need to celebrate themselves and everything that makes up who they are and know that they are enough.

Relevance

As learners move from a sense of belonging to a sense of believing, it is important to give them reflective space to identify the character traits, behaviors, strengths, and weaknesses they possess and for them to understand that all of those parts together are enough. Establish a place where learners are kind to themselves.

Learning Tools

- *I Am Enough,* by Grace Byers
- pencils, crayons, markers
- paper folded into four parts with headings in each quadrant, as shown below

Engage

Read aloud *I Am Enough.*

Build Knowledge

Choose examples of similes in the book and display them for the class to see; for example, "Like the sun, I'm here to shine." Ask learners: *What do you think the author means with these similes?* Explain that a *simile* is a figure of speech that compares two things using the word *like* or *as.* As you go through the text, share multiple examples of what the character in the story is being compared to.

I am . . . Like a . . .	I am . . . Like a . . .
I am . . . Like a . . .	I am . . . Like a . . .

Apply

1 Have learners brainstorm categories of objects they can be compared to. On the board or chart paper, list categories (colors, food, action verbs, animals, etc.) so that the whole group can see them.

2 Distribute the folded sheets of paper to learners. Have them complete the sentence frame *"I am _____ like a _____"* and illustrate each sentence. Encourage learners to list three strengths and one weakness.

Reflect

Invite learners to share their similes with the class. Encourage them to acknowledge both strengths and weaknesses as positive traits. Explain that knowing our weaknesses gives us something to work toward. Learners can compare strengths and weaknesses with classmates to illustrate similarities and differences and to understand that we are all diverse and we are all enough.

The Best of My Friend

Overview

Identifying what makes us different from one another is an important step in accepting others. Identifying strengths in others and moving from considering oneself to considering others provide a cornerstone for building a positive, inclusive, and affirming classroom culture.

Relevance

This lesson invites learners to collaborate and identify the attributes that make other people special. It allows children to explore different ways of giving encouragement through images and writing.

Learning Tools

- *The Best Part of Me,* by Wendy Ewald
- camera (or smartphone with camera function) and photo printer
- writing paper or word processor

Engage

Show learners a close-up photo of a part of your pet (for example, its paw) or of any animal. Tell learners: *This is the best part of my cat.* Ask: *What do you see? How would you describe it? Why do you think it is the best part?*

Share a prepared explanation; for example: *This is my cat Looey's paw. It is white like a fluffy cloud. He has sharp claws, but he doesn't use them on me. He uses his paws like love pillows. It's like he is kneading dough. This is the best part of Looey because he uses his paws like a cat hug on me.*

Build Knowledge

Before reading the book *The Best Part of Me*, share the images inside with learners. For young learners, body parts are always funny. Explain that you are going to

Close-up of my cat's paw

share a very special book created by children just like them. Each page focuses on something that child sees as the best part of him or her.

Read aloud *The Best Part of Me*. Pause throughout and ask: *Who thinks their eyes (or feet, or hair, etc.) are the best part of them? Why do you think that?*

After reading, review several photographs in the book. Explain the perspective used to take the photographs. Note that the images are black and white and are close-ups.

Apply

Tell learners that they are going to have the opportunity to identify the best part of a friend in class. They will take a picture and write about it. Remind learners there should be no inappropriate photographs. (Expectations always need to be reviewed with young learners!)

1 Partner up learners. (Decide how this will be orchestrated in your classroom.)

2 Have partners sit knee-to-knee and give them three minutes to look at each other. No talking. (Giggling is allowed!) Tell learners: *As you look at your partner, think about what is the best part that you see.*

3 Encourage partners to share aloud what they see as the best part of each other.

4 Using a camera or the camera function on a smartphone, have learners snap a photograph of the best part of their partner. Remind learners of the style in the book so their photograph mimic the same style.

5 Have learners print their photos and glue or tape it to a sheet of writing paper. Then have them write why they think that feature is the best part of their friend. Alternatively, learners can insert their photos in a word document and write about it.

Reflect

Publish the stories and create a class storybook. While sharing the class storybook, ask learners: *Did anyone have the same best part?* If so, note the subtle differences. For those things that are different, state how important it is to celebrate differences. While we are all different, we all have best parts and we all belong here!

Life's Little Equations

Overview

Understanding emotions is a challenge for young learners. Getting children to identify emotions and what they mean is important in promoting social confidence.

Relevance

This lesson explores emotions in an abstract context. It nudges learners to think about positive and negative emotions and how they can deal with them. It also provides a lens for teachers to see some implicit cues in their young learners.

Learning Tools

- *This Plus That: Life's Little Equations,* by Amy Krouse Rosenthal

- Life's Equation Think Sheet template (See example below; make it relevant for your learners.)

- paper for final product

Life's Equation Think Sheet

1. Let's practice an easy equation. Make an equation out of your name.

> **first name + middle name + last name = word that defines you**

2. What combination of words equals your best friend, pet, home, or family?

> _____ + _____ + _____ = **best friend**

3. What defines happiness or sadness for you?

> _____ + _____ + _____ = **happiness**

> _____ + _____ + _____ = **sadness**

4. What do you like about school?

> _____ + _____ + _____ = **school**

5. What do you worry about?

> _____ + _____ = **worry**

Create your own life equation out one of the following: strengths, weaknesses, hopes, worries. Write it below. Then pick your favorite and illustrate it.

Engage

Read aloud *This Plus That: Life's Little Equations*. While reading, cover up the sums to the equations in the book and encourage learners to guess the solutions. Accept learners' answers, even if they don't match the text.

Build Knowledge

Ask learners: *What is an equation?* (a number sentence) Say: *We just shared a story full of equations, but they were not made up of numbers. Can we broaden our idea of an equation?* (An equation can be mathematical, but it can also be the connection between other things, like the equations in the book.)

Apply

Using a Life's Equation Think Sheet, guide learners through each equation and solicit original answers. Then invite learners to create their own equations and illustrate them. Emphasize that the final equation should connect to emotions.

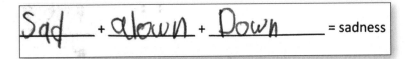

Two children's equations for sadness

Reflect

Share learners' equations and invite peers to offer feedback. Ensure you are using appropriate social-emotional expressions to build on in later lessons.

What If Everyone . . .

Overview

Establishing student-derived classroom rituals and routines creates space for young learners to use their voice and teaches them to be accountable for their role in the classroom community.

Relevance

This lesson builds positive classroom community by allowing each learner to recognize his or her belonging in the classroom. By understanding his or her important role, the standard of expectation becomes a collaborative one.

Learning Tools

- *If Everybody Did,* by Jo Ann Stover
- large index cards, one for each learner, with the heading "What if everyone . . ."

What if everyone . . .

Engage

Read aloud *If Everybody Did*. Ask learners: *What would really happen if everyone did what the illustrations show? How would the situation feel? How would it make you feel if you really didn't want to do something, but you had to do it anyway?*

Build Knowledge

Tell learners: *We must have expectations in our classroom. Since we all are part of this learning community, every one of us has a say in what is expected. Think about our classroom and what is important to you. Think about what it would look and feel like if the wrong things happened in the classroom. For example: What would happen if your teacher was never prepared to teach?*

Apply

Hand each learner a "What if everyone . . ." card and ask children to complete the sentence with something that would be detrimental to classroom life. For example, "What if everyone ran in the hallways?" or "What if everyone shouted their answers?" Guide learners to be purposeful in their thinking and writing. Explain that silly, outlandish ideas don't help create expectations.

Reflect

Invite each learner to share his or her "What if everyone . . ." response. Discuss what would happen if everyone did that thing and decide what expectation needs to be in place to ensure that it doesn't happen. For example: *If everybody ran in the school, lots of people would get hurt. So we need to be safe when we are moving from one place to the next.*

Find Your Voice

Raise your words, not voice. It is rain that grows flowers, not thunder.

—RUMI

Overview

Leaning into learners means listening. To listen, teachers need to ensure classrooms have a context in which learners can confidently use their voice to advocate for themselves, share their thinking, and ask for the support they need.

Relevance

This lesson invites learners to explore the meaning of voice as an intent. It helps create a context in which learners have confidence using their voice in cognitive and social settings.

Learning Tools

- *Cay and Adlee Find Their Voice,* by Cali and Russ Quaglia

- chart paper

- paper, cardstock, digital drawing tool, or any medium for learners to share a representation of their individual voice

Engage

Read aloud this quote from Rumi: *Raise your words, not voice. It is rain that grows flowers, not thunder.* Give learners a few minutes to share what they think the quote means. Allow several learners to share.

Build Knowledge

Tell learners: *We all have a voice. Our voice makes noise. But our voice also sends a message. No matter what our voice sounds like, we need to think of the message we are sending.*

One day in our classroom, a learner was drumming on the table with a pencil over and over and got on another learner's nerves. Instead of politely asking, "Will you please stop drumming on the table?" the second learner screamed, "Stop doing that! It is annoying!"

Tell learners: *We need to make sure we find our voice and use it to help us learn and grow. Let's meet two bird friends who are learning the message their voices can send.*

Read aloud *Cay and Adlee Find Their Voice*. Pause during certain scenarios and ask for real-life examples of when learners used the type of voice illustrated.

Apply

Have learners brainstorm the type of voice they have, keeping in mind intent, and reflect on a scenario when they might use that voice. Encourage learners to explore original words to represent their voice. For example, "I use a calm voice when there is an emergency." Invite each learner to write their type of voice on a chart paper, displayed for the class. This allows learners to see traits they have in common with their peers and reflect on their differences, too. It also illustrates that our voice can have a different intent depending on the situation. After brainstorming, provide learners with paper, cardstock, and other art supplies and invite them to create a visual representation of their personal voice using text and illustrations.

A learner describes her voice.

Reflect

Invite learners to share their voice choice and collect every learner's visual representation into a class book. Remind learners that our voice message can change depending on the context. For example, we may use an excited voice when we have just won a prize, but we wouldn't use that same voice to explain why we didn't have our materials for school.

Different Perspectives

Overview

Learning how to take on a different perspective allows learners to explore empathy.

Relevance

Empathy is a social-emotional trait that nudges learners to see outside of themselves. It is a place that reinforces listening with more than our ears. Empathy promotes implicit understanding between peers.

Learning Tools

- image of rabbit-duck illusion (see right; search online)

- small sticky notes

- *They All Saw a Cat,* by Brendan Wenzel

- *"Sesame Street:* Mark Ruffalo: Empathy" video on YouTube (https://www.youtube.com/watch?v=9_1Rt1R4xbM)

- various images that show situations that could tap into a young learner's emotions (for example, a lost teddy bear on the side of a road, a child alone on a playground, a child not wanting to eat broccoli)

Engage

Give each learner a small sticky note. Display the rabbit-duck image on the board and ask learners to write down what they see, without talking. Call on a learner to share what he or she sees. Ask the class who else saw the same thing. (Young learners often will see things that teachers cannot see, and that's okay!) Guide the conversation to see if everyone can see either the duck or the rabbit or both.

Explain that the word *perspective* means "a particular way of looking at a situation," often from a different point of view. It requires you to put yourself in another person's position and imagine what you would feel, think, or do if you were in that situation. Explain that perspective shapes what we see.

Build Knowledge

Read aloud *They All Saw a Cat*. Pause after each page to ask learners to identify each perspective. Emphasize how the perspective changes by asking:

- *How does the child see the cat?* (The child sees the cat as caring, friendly, a pet, cuddly. Note: Allow students to infer before showing the illustration.)

- *How does the dog see the cat?* (The dog sees the cat as a weaker animal, a nuisance, a pest.)

- *How has the perspective changed?* (Emphasize that the cat did not change. The author and illustrator changed the illustrations to represent the change in perspective, but the cat itself did not change. You will have to repeat this often, especially for younger learners.)

- *How does the fox see the cat?* (The fox sees the cat as something to eat, as prey. The cat did not change; only the perspective did.)

- *How does the fish see the cat?* (The fish sees the cat as something really big. It sees the cat through the glass bowl and water, which makes the cat look blurry.)

- *How does the mouse see the cat?* (The mouse sees the cat as a ferocious predator—mean and scary.)

- *How does the bee see the cat?* (Some children may say "in dots." Explain that bees have five eyes and when they see things, it looks like these illustrations. Say: *Imagine looking through the ends of a handful of drinking straws—this is what it would look like.* Did the cat suddenly turn into a grouping of dots? No. The animal seeing the cat had a different perspective.)

- *How does the bird see the cat?* (The bird sees the cat from what we call a *bird's-eye view*, which means from up high—it sees something from above. Some children may say the bird sees the cat as a predator. You may want to point out that the cat isn't even aware of the bird. Remember, we don't want to assume what the cat thinks about the bird.)

- *How does the flea see the cat?* (The flea sees the cat as something really, really big, as something to feed on.)

- *How does the snake see the cat?* (Some children may say the snake sees the cat in bright colors. Share that snakes see "heat" in primary colors. The snake may see the cat as something larger or may just know that something is there. Did the cat suddenly change color? No, the way the cat is seen is what has changed.)

- *How does the skunk see the cat?* (The illustrator shows the skunk seeing the cat in black and white. Skunks have very poor eyesight. The skunk knows it has a good self-defense mechanism with his spray, so it may not feel threatened by the cat.)

- *How does the earthworm see the cat?* (Earthworms don't see. They feel vibrations in the ground. The earthworm senses the cat as something very large. The illustrator made little vibratory lines to make it look like the cat is walking on top of the earthworm. Did the cat disappear and just become a noise? No, the worm "sees" the cat differently because its perspective is different.)

- *How does the bat see the cat?* (The bat may "see" the cat as a threat, but bats don't see with their eyes. Ask learners: *Does anyone know what bats use to see?* Bats use echolocation— they emit, or give off, sound waves and wait for the echo. Maybe the bat sees the cat as something to play with, to bug, or to be wary of.)

- *How does the cat see itself? Does the cat see itself the way anyone else sees it?* (No, the cat sees itself differently, too. That is perspective.)

Apply

Connect the word *perspective* to empathy.

1 Ask learners: *Have you ever been with a friend who got a new toy, and he is so excited about it, and you feel yourself getting excited even though you didn't get a toy at the same time? You feel excited because you know what it feels like to get a new toy. That is empathy.*

2 Show learners the video *"Sesame Street:* Mark Ruffalo: Empathy" on YouTube.

3 Ask: *How did Murray feel when Mark Ruffalo stubbed his toe?* (Murray felt in his heart what Mark felt in his toe, even though he didn't hurt his own toe. That is empathy.) *How did Murray feel when Mark told him about his lost teddy bear?* (Murray could imagine how Mark felt when he lost his teddy bear, even though he didn't lose his own teddy bear—that is empathy!)

Reflect

One by one, share the images you collected to tap into young learners' emotions. Discuss each image, eliciting how children feel about it. For example, show an image of a child on a swing by himself. Possible response: "I feel sad for the boy." Ask: *Why?* Possible response: "Because he is alone." Say: *You aren't alone, so why do you feel sad?* Invite learners to express either in writing or verbally why empathy is an important trait to develop.

Take Flight

Overview

Teaching young learners to believe in themselves and trust their own abilities can be challenging. Teachers need to reinforce the self-direction and self-reliance it takes for young learners to be persistent and fly through challenges and soar toward aspirations.

Relevance

This lesson invites young learners to observe what can happen when someone thinks you aren't capable of doing something you think you are able to do. It establishes the notion of resilience and persistence and believing in oneself, even if no one else does.

Learning Tools

- "Penguins Can Fly" video on BBC (https://www.bbc.co.uk/programmes/p00l80w2)

- *Flight School,* by Lita Judge

- "Chaos Box" materials (A hodgepodge of consumable materials for creative projects. If you don't have materials, the task can be paper and pencil, too.)

- paper for learners to share a representation of thinking, if they choose not to create an artifact

"Chaos Boxes" hold random materials that can be used for any project.

Engage

Show children the video "Penguins Can Fly."

Build Knowledge

Say to learners: *Penguins can't fly. Why did the narrator in the video say penguins can fly?* (It looked like they were flying.) *Have you ever wondered if penguins can't fly just because we don't believe they can? I mean, what if we all just started to believe they could—would they be able to fly?* (Responses will vary; make the leap with your learners that even if we don't think penguins can, there is power in believing they can.) *Those penguins looked to me like they were flying. I bet they felt like they were flying, too.*

Read aloud *Flight School*. Where appropriate, talk about Penguin's belief in his ability to fly. Prompt learners:

- *How do we know he believes in himself?*
- *Do his teachers believe he can fly?*
- *Do his friends believe he can fly?*
- *Why does Penguin believe he can fly?*

Pause the read-aloud after the part in which Penguin's teachers give up on him and are unsure what to do. Do not let learners see Flamingo's idea. Ask: *What can we do to help Penguin?*

Apply

Challenge learners to invent a way to help Penguin fly—either through a sketch or by building something. Many learners will lean toward a flying contraption of some sort. Remind them of the video and that although penguins cannot fly, they can feel like they are flying. Have them consider that in their designs. After learners create, allow them to share their ideas.

Reflect

Finish reading *Flight School* and have learners reflect on the following questions:

- *What does it feel like when no one believes in you?*
- *Why is believing in yourself important?*
- *What can you do to learn to believe in yourself when things are challenging?*

What's in a Name?

Overview

Our name is an important piece of our identity. It can reveal family cultural values.

Relevance

This lesson invites learners to explore the meaning of their names and interview family members about their names.

Learning Tools

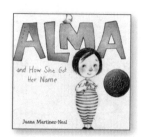

- *Alma and How She Got Her Name,* by Juana Martinez-Neal
- letters from learners' grown-ups*
- websites or books on etymology for learners to further research the meaning of their names
- half sheet of cardstock or paper for each learner

* Prior to this lesson, solicit grown-ups to write a letter to their child explaining the story of their name. Explain the task to grown-ups and ask them to type or handwrite the letter (using print, not cursive) so that young learners can read it. Ask grown-ups to send the letter directly to you so it is a surprise for the lesson. For grown-ups who do not participate, create a story for that child based on the etymology of his or her name.

Engage

Share with your learners your first name and the meaning of your name. If you know why your family chose your name, share that story, too.

Build Knowledge

Read aloud *Alma and How She Got Her Name.*

Apply

After reading, give learners the letters about their names. As they read their letters, help learners look up the meaning of their names. Learners will create a nameplate incorporating the meaning and the story of their name. Give each child a half sheet of cardstock or paper. Guide learners to include the following on their half sheet:

- name
- meaning
- illustration that represents the meaning (For example, a name that means "strong" may be written with very bold letters with muscles drawn on the first letter of the name; a name that means "shining one" may be illustrated with stars.)

Reflect

Encourage learners to share their nameplate and the short story of their name with the class. Use the nameplates throughout the year for grouping purposes, when visitors visit the classroom, or as part of a classroom display.

Working Together

Overview

Learning to collaborate can be challenging for young learners. Children are egocentric and often have a hard time compromising when it comes to ideas and shared responsibility in learning.

Relevance

This lesson illustrates what happens when we don't work together and we only want to do things our way. Learners need to identify and focus on working to their strengths while trying to improve their weaknesses.

Learning Tools

- *Up the Creek,* by Nicholas Oldland
- chart paper and marker

Engage

Ask learners: *Have you ever heard the phrase, "Up the creek without a paddle?" What does that mean? Imagine being on a canoe in a creek and suddenly losing your paddle. What would happen?*

Build Knowledge

Read aloud *Up the Creek.* During the read aloud, solicit responses about what is happening in the story and why. (The animals all want to do the same thing; they all want to do it their way; no one is listening; and so on.)

Apply

On chart paper, create a T-chart with the headings "Looks Like" and "Sounds Like." Ask learners: *What does good teamwork look like? What does it sound like?* List their responses on the chart.

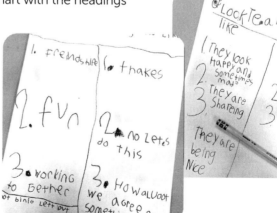

Have children describe what teamwork looks and sounds like.

Teamwork

LOOKS LIKE . . .	SOUNDS LIKE . . .
Using resources the way they are meant to be used	Hearing all ideas
Sharing of ideas	Getting along
Working together	Working in a nice inside, kind voice
Following a plan	Collaborating
Taking turns	Friendship
Getting the job done	Using kind words
Joining in	Using your ideas
Listening to each other	Compromising
Sharing materials	Using your voice
Fun!	Asking for things nicely
Not being left out	A plan (it is ordered)
Letting others do things	Trusting your team
Kindness	"I believe in you!"
When something doesn't go right, try again!	
Go, Brain!	

Reflect

Invite learners to reflect on what makes them a good team member and what makes them a poor team member.

Afterword

In the rush to return to normal, use this time to consider which parts of normal are worth rushing back to.

—DAVE HOLLIS

Relevant matters are enduring. While popular culture fads and young learners' interests may change over time, the significant moments that shape them do not change. Consider the spring of 2020. If you worked in education during that time, you experienced a pivot like none we had experienced before. In my own teaching environment, within 24 hours, my colleagues and I found ourselves teaching in an entirely new context. Our experiences in technology integration simply were not enough for us to feel confident about navigating what became crisis teaching in a virtual context. By the time we returned to teaching after the pandemic, educators once again had to pivot into a defined context of virtual teaching and learning. I believe that for the many teachers and children who celebrated success more than mourned the shift in teaching and learning, it was in large part due to their awareness and engagement with the most relevant matters: leaning in, understanding learners, tackling emotionality, treasuring culture, looking around, and exploring authentic experiences. The views presented in this book can be applied beyond a brick-and-mortar classroom. The execution may look different, but conceptually, teachers should consider the ideas in any kind of educational setting.

Every day throughout the pandemic, we forged relationships behind our screens. They were relationships built on engagement and high expectations and belief. In a digital sphere, we learned to communicate,

"You belong here." It meant spending more time discussing and establishing routines. We had to be patient and improve our understanding. Many of us got glimpses into our learners' lives that we hadn't had before. We had to tackle emotionality. Sometimes it was our own or our colleagues', but our learners were also dealing with many issues in addition to navigating a digital approach to learning.

Teachers had to look around and be aware of the current things happening in the world and help bring the joyful parts of an insecure world to our learners.

We had to be aware of those needs and design ways to embrace cultural differences alongside an already challenging academic situation. Littles were missing their extended families and not celebrating their birthdays with friends. Relevance changed for learners since they weren't participating in hobbies as freely, if at all. Teachers had to look around and be aware of what was happening in the world and help bring the joyful parts of that insecure world. We still had to build experiences and not let digital learning be the defining experience of our students' school year. As one of the teachers who went through this shift in teaching, I am confident that while my methodologies may have been less inspiring, my digital prowess often lacking, and my facilitation of 20 young learners on a computer sometimes less than proficient, the time we spent together was relevant and mattered.

As we return to normal and as your own repertoire continues to expand, examine your intentions with young learners and ask: *Am I equipped to explore the issues that really matter? What is the payoff if I do? What are the consequences if I do not? Even more important, do I foster a sense of belonging? Do I establish a place for believing? And, ultimately, do my learners strive to become who they want to be?*

Acknowledgments

The creation of *Make It Relevant!* has been encouraged by so many people. I have always typed in the word *author* when I needed to input "my dream job" on a computer screen. ("Teacher" was something I had already attained.) With this book, my dream job was fulfilled. I guess I'll have to think of a new aspiration now. While this is the end of the book, it is, quite honestly, the most difficult part to write. These pages are a record of nearly 21 years in education, but a lifetime of being in love with learning.

First, I need to thank my husband, Robbie: Your constant encouragement, belief, patience, endless ear, and advice. Your cups of tea aren't bad either. My daughter, Chloe: When you became a teacher, I knew your students were in for a real treat. Little did I know the benefit I would get from seeing education through your eyes. I adore our conversations and watching you thrive to be relevant with your learners every single day. My son, Rory: I wrote these words with your early school experiences in mind. Had your teachers been more relevant, they would have captured what an amazing, confident, kind, and talented young man you are. It might be time to get those matching tattoos. To my brother, Jonathan, my silent encourager: When I told you this was happening, your reaction made me feel so loved. For my momma: No matter what, you cheer me on. You have told me for years, "you need to write a book." Well, here it is. My daddy: You instilled in me the love of words, so every word that I penned on these pages has your heart print on them.

I must also recognize my professional family. There have been many educators who have cheered me on, challenged me to do more for the kids, and encouraged me to use my voice to steer education toward a place that resonates with joy and meaning for all of us.

Mr. Frank Stronge was my cooperating teacher when I was student teaching. I will never forget the morning I was juggling volumes of state standards bound in books and getting ready to plan my teaching unit. He looked at me and said, "What are you doing with those?" I replied, "Well, I need to plan my unit that I am going to teach." He shook his head, took the volumes from me, and said, "No. You don't start here. Go ask the kids what they want to learn." I never stopped doing that. Thank you, Frank.

Other colleagues who have become friends and appreciate my constant sense of wanting to do more for my Littles are the "Bigs," whom I lean into often: Dawn, for being my work wife and adopting me as a teammate; Kendra, your servant leader heart for teachers is one of the boldest I've known; Lisa, your lens on curriculum and creating engagement from the simplest notions make it so much fun to collaborate with you—let's start that podcast; Cindy, you always try things I'm encouraging you to try—even though I'm sure you still give kids candy; Michelle, I'm thankful for witnessing the high expectations you have for yourself and your learners; Monica A., one of the most positive, encouraging people in my balcony, your thoughtful words and notes have lifted me at times when you didn't even know I needed them; Nancy, I've never worked with someone as creative as you—I love how you see the world, and it all funnels into teaching; Julia, "Siri, call Valerie . . ."—the laughs we have shared are some of the best; Sandra, your teacher heart is buried in the ideas in this book—you just "get it" and I am thankful; Nakasha, thanks for keeping me current on my shoe game—try to catch me; Renea, I've loved our daily early morning chats and the fact that you let me go on and on about cats and take good care of Einstein; Anne and Melanie, you have listened to me, commiserated with me, celebrated with me—I am grateful we are connected through education; Angela, Beth, Karen R., and Meg, our group chats have given me life when my teacher tank was empty—you always share your perspective, whether it is school, politics, swearing, or dogs versus cats; Beth, I can't wait for your red annotations on this—be kind!

I have had many administrators who allowed me to be that offbeat, boundary-pushing educator. Sarah K., Belinda, Keeli, Cissi, Brett, Sharon, Katrina, and my very first principal, Mr. Eddie Spears. I still remember the day Mr. Spears showed me my classroom. There was a portable wall between two rooms, and I said, "Well, since no one is on the other side, just let me have both rooms." He did, and I used them well. I am proud to have served alongside all of you.

This book would not have been possible without a giant nudge from Dave Burgess. We spoke after a professional learning experience, and he told me to write. He encouraged me to start with a blog and tell my story. Thank you, Dave, for getting me to use my voice and leading many of us to ways that matter most.

Denis Sheeran, I thank you for taking time that afternoon in Atlanta to brainstorm with me. You continue to share ideas that bring relevance to my teaching. You now have a group of Littles who are constantly looking for impostor snowflakes.

Dr. Ashley Kennedy, who would have realized all those years ago when we were sitting in a computer lab together—two "word girls" trying to figure out numbers and statistics—that this would be the result? You are impeccable with your word and your intent. My own words will never match the gratitude I have for your faith in me and your support of me through this project.

My Littles and their grown-ups deserve recognition. Without them, there are no relevant matters. This book is us. It is about us, and it is for us. It is the challenges, the chaos, the laughter, and the learning we have shared. Each of you has a part in this story. I thank you for letting me tell it this way.

Finally, the team at Scholastic: Maria L. Chang, Tara Welty, Tannaz Fassihi, and all the crew. I remember poring over my Scholastic book-order form when I was a little girl. I would circle and recircle book choices, trying to make sure I purchased as many books as possible with my allowance. Now, here I am, writing for a company that always kept me reading, writing, and wondering. I thank you for trusting me to use my voice to tell a story that needs to be told.

References

Beloit College. (2014). Mindset lists: 2018 list. http://themindsetlist.com/lists/the-mindset-list-for-the-class-of-2018-born-in-1996/

Bloom, B. S. (1956). *Taxonomy of educational objectives, handbook I: The cognitive domain.* New York, NY: David McKay Co. Inc.

Cain, S. (2012). *Quiet: The power of introverts in a world that can't stop talking.* New York, NY: Broadway Books.

Christakis, E. (2017). *The importance of being little: What preschoolers really need from grown-ups.* New York, NY: Penguin Books.

Collaborative for Academic, Social, and Emotional Learning. (2012). Effective social and emotional learning programs: Preschool and elementary school edition. https://casel.org/wp-content/uploads/2016/01/2013-casel-guide-1.pdf

Daniels, H. (2017). *The curious classroom: 10 structures for teaching with student-directed inquiry.* Portsmouth, NH: Heinemann.

De Houwer, J. (2019). Implicit bias is behavior: A functional-cognitive perspective on implicit bias. *Perspectives on Psychological Science, 14,* 835–840.

Department of Education, Employment and Workplace Relations. (2009). Belonging, being and becoming: The early years learning framework for Australia. https://www.acecqa.gov.au/sites/default/files/2018-02/belonging_being_and_becoming_the_early_years_learning_framework_for_australia.pdf

Dewey, J. (1916). *Democracy and education: An introduction to the philosophy of education.* New York, NY: Macmillan.

Druckerman, P. (2012). *Bringing up bebe: One American mother discovers the wisdom of French parenting.* New York, NY: Penguin Press.

Dusenbury, L., & Weissberg R. P. (2017). Social emotional learning in elementary school: Preparations for success. Edna Bennett Pierce Prevention Research Center, Pennsylvania State University.

Fay, J. & Funk, D. (1995). *Teaching with love and logic: Taking control of the classroom.* Golden, CO: Love and Logic Press.

Ginott, H. (1972). *Teacher and child: A book for parents and teachers.* New York, NY: The Macmillan Company.

Gray, P. (2011). The decline of play and the rise of psychopathology in children and adolescents. *American Journal of Play, 3*(4), 443–463.

Hattie, J. (2012). *Visible learning for teachers: Maximizing impact on learning.* New York, NY: Routledge.

Klein, A. (2002). Infant and toddler care that recognizes their competence: Practices at the Pikler Institute. *Dimensions of Early Childhood, 2,* 11–18.

Kriete, R. & Bechtel, L. (2002). *The morning meeting book.* Greenfield, MA: Northeast Foundation for Children.

Ladson-Billings, G. (1994). *The dreamkeepers.* San Francisco, CA: Jossey-Bass Publishing Co.

Lynch, M. (2015). More play, please: The perspective of kindergarten teachers on play in the classroom. *American Journal of Play, 7*(3), 347–370.

Marzano, R., Pickering, J., & Heflebower, T. (2010). *The highly engaged classroom: The classroom strategies series (Generating high levels of student attention and engagement).* Bloomington, IN: Marzano Research Laboratory.

Mitra, D. (2008). *Student voice in school reform: Building youth-adult partnerships that strengthen schools and empower youth.* Albany, NY: State University of New York Press.

National Scientific Council on the Developing Child. (2004). Young children develop in an environment of relationships: Working paper no. 1. Retrieved from http://developingchild.harvard.edu/wp-content/uploads/2004/04/Young-Children-Develop-in-an-Environment-of-Relationships.pdf

Nicholson, S. (2009). The theory of Loose Parts: An important principle for design methodology. *Studies in Design Education Craft & Technology, 4*(2), 5–14.

Paul, A. (2012, March 17). Your brain on fiction. *The New York Times.* Retrieved from https://www.nytimes.com/2012/03/18/opinion/sunday/the-neuroscience-of-your-brain-on-fiction.html

Pinto, C. (2019, August 5). Social and emotional learning through children's literature. Global Partnership for Education. https://www.globalpartnership.org/blog/social-and-emotional-learning-through-childrens-literature

Quaglia, R., Fox, K., Lande, L., & Young, D. (2020). *The power of voice in schools: Listening, learning and leading together.* Alexandria, VA: ASCD.

Roberts, S. & Crawford, P. (2008). Literature to help children cope with family stressors. *Young Children, 63*(5), 12–17.

Silverstein, L., & Layne, S. (2010). Defining arts integration. The John F. Kennedy Center for the Performing Arts. Retrieved from https://www.kennedy-center.org/globalassets/education/resources-for-educators/classroom-resources/artsedge/article/arts-integration-resources/what-is-arts-integration/definingartsintegration.pdf

Steel, J. (2016). Noncognitive factors in an elementary school-wide arts integrated model. *Journal for Learning through the Arts: A Research Journal on Arts Integration in Schools and Communities, 12*(1), Retrieved from https://escholarship.org/uc/item/4611h6w3

UK Essays. (November 2018). Importance of schedule and routine for young children. Retrieved from https://www.ukessays.com/essays/young-people/importance-of-schedule-and-routine-for-young-children-young-people-essay.php?vref=1